CLASS WAR

A Decade of DISORDER

Edited by
Ian Bone,
Alan Pullen &
Tim Scargill

VERSO

London · New York

First published by VERSO 1991
© Verso 1991
All rights reserved

ISBN 0 86091 5581
ISBN 978-0-86091-558-4
Verso
UK: 6 Meard Street,London W1V 3HR
USA: 29 West 35th Street, New York
 NY 10001-2291

British Library Cataloguing
in Publication Data and US Library
of Congress Cataloguing in
Publication Data available.

Graphic production: Paul Elliman

Printed and bound
in the United Kingdom

Dedicated to
the ram-raiders
& rioters of
September '91-
who have done
more for our
class than 1000
labour party
resolutions.

CLASS ANGER HAS [REDACTED]

CLASS ANGER HAS ERUPTED.We're not gonna stay sulking away in our estates and ghettos,schools,factories and dole queues,out of sight and out of mind any longer...We are on the WARPATH.At Henley regatta the hordes of rich parasites were made to feel our hatred,to see the first STORMCLOUDS on their horizon.We fucked up their day just as they fuckup our lives from the cradle to the grave.

But Henley,like all the other toffy-nosed social events,is just a carnival of their swanky lifestyles - the BASTARDS always remain safe behind the doors of their mansions. Now is the time to turn the tables and fight back.We're gonna take the CLASS WAR to their fuckin doorsteps.

Hampstead is the largest target for the BASH THE RICH offensive.Hampstead,London's poshest borough...where the millionaire elite live it up while we have to struggle to make ends meet, basking in their grand mansions and indoor swimming pools,cruising around in their rollers;growing fat from the cash they've screwed out of the workingclass and laughing til they choke on their crystal glasses,overflowing with champagne,at how

they've shat on us. Where middleclass radicals and trendy lefties smarmaway their days eating quiche lorraine,sipping Perrier water and mouthing off about "the nasty atomic bomb" and "terrible Third World famine" while under their very noses people are living on the streets and in shitty housing in the depths of poverty, and pensioners freeze to death in their squalid bedsit hellholes.

Where the states soft cops - social workers,teachers,judges and all that scummy shower dwell in isolation from the people whose interests they either claim "to hold at heart"or have the power to lock in prison or put into care.

Well SHITBAGS,your days are numbered.We've lived our lives up to our necks in your shit and now its your turn to suffer,to feel the brunt of our class anger and hatred.We won't be fooled by the sickening smoke-screen of the Labour party,the left and the unions. The only Politics with meaning for us are on the streets and we will not rest til we've got our own back on these bastards.

GET BARRICADING THAT DOORWAY SCUMBAGS!

ERUPTED

DISORDER Is Our POWER

This book celebrates ten years of vibrant working class resistance in Britain – a decade when the ungovernable class, both in daily life and pitched street battles, continually gave the lie to the consensus middle ground politics of Tory and Labour. In ten years that the end of the working class was predicted by left and right alike, by Thatcher, Major and Kinnock, that same ungovernable class conspicuously failed to read its obituary notice.

In 1981 riots seared like wildfire around the country, rendering city centres no-go areas for the police and spreading to county towns and dreaming spires. From Toxteth to Tunbridge Wells the blissful hot summer of 1981 smouldered and ignited as whole communities rose up.

In 1990 uprisings against the poll tax erupted outside every council chamber and shire hall culminating in that glorious carnival of insurrection at Trafalgar Square when 10,000 riotous working class heroes were cheered by another 200,000 as they torched buildings, fought cops with scaffolding poles, and brought the reality of class war to the cossetted rich of the West End. Downing Street escaped storming by a hair's breadth as the fresh memory of Ceaucescu's downfall inspired thousands to believe that Thatcher could meet the same fate. In a way she did – millions of non-payers resisting court orders and bailiffs made her Poll Tax uncollectable and consigned it, and her, to the dustbin.

For a supposedly strong government with a subdued working class, the Tories were having a lot of trouble making their rule stick. The defeat of the poll tax by popular resistance followed the collapse of the football supporters' ID scheme and plans for Housing Action Trusts on council estates. We, the working class, stopped these initiatives by our physical power on the streets, estates and terraces. The government could no more control its legislative programme than it could enforce rule in the inner cities where the cops feared to go unless in convoys of riot vans. The 1985 uprisings in Handsworth, Brixton and Tottenham saw whole communities pounding the cops to defeat. Who could forget the look of incomprehending fear which flitted across the face of Douglas Hurd as he was stoned in Handsworth or the phoney blustering of David Waddington when jostled and

spat at in Central London?

The miners' strike saw unprecedentedly ferocious class warfare spilling across the whole country – the pitched battles at Orgreave and Mansfield, the self-organization of hit squads as they wreaked havoc on NCB property throughout the coalfields, the ungovernability of the pit villages of South Yorkshire where the only authority was the raw class power of the miners themselves. The Tories' writ ran no larger in Maltby and Grimethorpe than in Crossmaglen. Nightly battles raged outside Stalag Wapping whilst, nearby in London's docklands, yuppie bashing became a popular local pastime and rich newcomers were forced to protect themselves with security guards and barbed wire to prevent local youth exacting a 'yuppie tax'. So much for the Labour-Tory axis of consensus in a classless society.

Before Andy Murphy of *Class War* said on television that the Trafalgar Square rioters were working class heroes the interviewer warned that 'some viewers may find these opinions offensive' Bollocks! Not the millions who stared with disbelief and joy at their TV screens because at last someone had the bottle to say what they thought. The imaginary consensus constructed by the media, that everyone was a law abiding, forelock tugging respect-your-betters moderate was exploded by the popularity of police bashing as both an urban and rural Saturday night pastime. When the Grand Hotel in Brighton was blown up millions of working class people devoutly cursed that Thatcher had escaped and got stuck into their bacon and eggs with joyful gusto as TV screens showed Tebbit submerged in the wreckage.

Despite the media's grovelling to the Royal family, expecting us to share their sycophantic joy at Fergie's ski slope cavortings, the Windsors and their hangers-on were roundly damned as parasitic wasters in working class homes throughout the country. Hundreds of thousands squatted empty flats and houses rather than tolerate the absurdity of bed and breakfasts or council waiting lists. The nation's army of shoplifters did much to redress economic inequality – shopping without money finding its ultimate expression in the ram raiders' joyous trashing of luxury cars. Pitch invasions by football fans thwarted the merger dreams of many a smug club chairman. Holiday homes continued to blaze merrily in North

Wales where ten years of fruitless police investigation were frustrated by the community's total silence. Bengali and Asian youth told respectable community leaders to fuck off with their whining about lack of police action on racist attacks. They organised their own community defence campaigns and recognised the wisdom of getting your retaliation in first. In 1986 and 1990, culminating in the Strangeways uprising, the prisons erupted. Not even in its own belly could the state guarantee law and order. For many of the dispossessed working class the loss of community or solidarity at work was re-created in those fleeting adrenalin moments of confrontation or riot when they fought as one with complete strangers, shared ammunition, built barricades, hugged and laughed and cursed as the fighting ebbed and flowed.

Thatcher's whispered remark following her 1987 election victory that 'we must do something about the inner cities' was no philanthropic gesture. It was an acknowledgement, after the '81 and '85 riots, that these remaining areas of working class solidarity were a physical threat to her survival. The Tories' solution was widespread social engineering and policing by design rather than overt repression. The Urban Development Councils homed in on any derelict dockland wharf or canalside adjacent to the city centre and paved the way for yuppie invasions. Inspector Pearman in Notting Hill discovered it was easier to close down the Mangrove by turning it into a wine bar than by endless drug raids. The buzzing front lines of '85 were, by '91, colonized by artists' galleries and picture framers, without a copper in sight. Dispossessed, the working class was shipped off to reservations in Basildon or Basingstoke.

The ID cards scheme, the ending of standing on the terraces and the introduction of executive boxes were intended to do for football what yuppies had done for Docklands. Do-it-yourself acid house parties quickly followed the Notting Hill carnival, free festivals and outdoor rock concerts as gatherings where the potential for disorder meant they had to be banned or turned into dead events in all seater stadia run by the cops. Outdoor drinking in city centres was outlawed. Curfews were introduced to try to stop large groups attacking the police after night club chucking out time. The only occasions when the working class could regain control of their own

territory were outlawed.

The spectre of violent disorder was continually raised to justify a massive extension of police activity. The inner cities, football grounds, acid house raves and hippy convoys were all full of bloodthirsty people who had to be policed out of existence. Can there be a more ludicrous image of the 1980s than the thousands of paramilitary police guarding Stonehenge at the behest of English Heritage from the presence of the only people for whom the stones still had any meaning?

Along with this inculcated fear of disorder went carefully constructed media myths that the working class was never lawless – trouble was always caused by a handful of 'outsiders'. The *Daily Express* claimed that the '81 riots were caused by three people on motorbikes travelling around the country. The *Daily Mail* exclusively revealed that people with foreign sounding accents had been overhead at a bus queue in North London following the Broadwater Farm riot. 'Non-miners' caused the trouble during the miners' strike, football hooligans weren't 'real' football fans, acid house parties were organised by drug barons, and agitators toured pubs offering punters £20

to join the poll tax riots. Meanwhile our 'own' working class was sitting at home eating fish and chips, drinking carry-outs from the off licence, watching satellite tv and never gathering in threatening numbers on the street unless led astray by 'outsiders'.

Unable to counter the loony baa baa white sheep tags of the media, the entire left offloaded its agenda and hightailed it for the centre ground. Kinnock and Hattersley tried to out-Thatcher the Tories in their commitment to law and order, deploring all law breaking up to and including the evasion of tv licenses. Non-payment and violent street demonstrations could never defeat the poll tax – for that we had to wait for the election of a Labour government. Paralysed to the point where they could say nothing that the media would construe as extreme, the Cunningham/Gould waxwork dummies spouted endless empty slogans about 'Opportunity Britain' and 'Our children's children's children'. Militant, too, were stronger on law and order than the Tories and promised on television to name the poll tax rioters. The Communist Party dissolved itself and its leading theoretician, Bea Campbell, became the country's foremost exposer

of satanic covens. The collapse of Soviet style communism was a large and overdue nail in the coffin of the Leninists. In the real world the left had quite simply gone down the plughole.

Part of the left's problem was that it failed to come to terms with the move away from the organization of the working class in the workplace. The terrain of class warfare was changing fast. The rapid decline in traditionally militant heavy industries such as coal and steel meant that the struggle in the workplace was no longer central. The left continued its' motion passing in NALGO and demanding this, that or the other of the TUC, but the punters didn't give a toss.

Just as closing down the pits had been more effective than baton charges in dealing with miners' guerilla warfare, so gentrification proved more effective than the use of snatch squads in quelling iner city resistance.

Pushed out of the city centres, it is on the large council estates where the working class are unleashing the most ferocious class warfare yet seen. The battle to control that territory – to keep the police out – has been going on in 'slow rioting' for years on estates from Glasgow to Plymouth. But now feet are stretching, literally, for the accelerator. Ram-raiding and joy-riding, and subsequent battles against the cops, are the real expression of class war in 1991. As the youth centres and shopping malls go up in smoke, the left can only gasp with incomprehension. The rioters are making no demands that the left can mediate – the sheer joy of the action is an end in itself. The increased sophistication of tactics – taking generators out to make looting easier, chopping down trees and telegraph poles with chain saws to make barricades, disrupting police communication with jamming equipment, firing flares at helicopters – are a joy to behold. Oxford, Cardiff, Handsworth and North Shields in the early Autumn of '91 are but the first shots in the soon to be fought battles that will rage the length and breadth of Britain. Battles in the community – over control of territory, space and time – have become the pivotal point of today's struggle.

The only paper that reflected this new battleground was *Class War*. The ungovernability of our class was celebrated in its pages whenever and wherever it broke out. *Class War* offered no apologies for class combativ-

Decade of DISORDER 9

ity, no excuses for class warfare, no explanations based on leftist bleating about homes, jobs and how nasty the police were. We knew all that already. We didn't need some middle class jerk of a Trotskyist to take us through the 'stages of history' or tell us about 'transitional demands' which could never be met. We didn't need it because we *were* working class – our politics was lived as a part of our everyday lives, not treated as a hobby like train spotting or hang gliding. The working class don't need their heads filled up with propaganda to make them revolutionary – to follow the eternal flame of the correct line – they know what is needed instinctively. All they lack is confidence in their collective combativity, autonomy and ability to win after years of defeatist bleatings and apologetics. To increase this confidence *Class War* had to act as well as talk. 'Action is the lifeblood – without action you're just posing' as one class warrior succinctly put it.

We didn't just reassert the solidarity of our communities, we took part in the struggle. There are no 'outsiders' in the working class and we poured into outbreaks of class warfare wherever they occurred. Riots, strikes, community defences, tea dances – we were there with a petrol bomb in one hand, a paper in the other, and a big smile on our faces. We reported the great eruptions but the paper was full of snippets about everyday struggle too. In the run down inner cities where our class was turned in on itself we fought against resignation and passivity, rejecting the dead end of anti-social crime and dog-eat-dog. We fought back against those who preyed on their own class pointing instead to the posh bastards guzzling Indonesian seaweed at cozy little brasseries on the other side of town.

Our politics encompassed the whole of life. Politics was to be enjoyed, for a laugh, for a good time day by day. We were not a dull sect flogging unread papers on street corners like Jehovah's witnesses. We weren't Marxist professors dressed up in donkey jackets, SWPers trying to flog papers to rampaging miners at Orgreave, or Militant grassing up the working class at Trafalgar Square. We were not a cult with the scientific truth up our sleeves. We understood the revolutionary process and we wanted

DISORDER Is Our POWER

When the rioters of Elswick and Scotswood threatened to spill down Westgate on the night of Friday September 13th, the panic in the posh shops of the city centre was as if the Goths were poised for the second sacking of Rome...

it to lead to the storming of Downing Street and Buckingham Palace. But we weren't going to be good boys and girls, minding our ps and qs until that great day came. For us the class war was about daily combativity, about collective action wherever possible. We were going to be ungovernable right now . . . and so was our class.

Born out of the riots of 1981, *Class War* has been at the forefront of the decade of disorder, bucking, rioting, rearing up, snarling, fighting tooth and nail for our class. We are dismissed as a joke by the left – scared shitless by a working class organization which was not dominated by the middle class and was not frightened by the sweat, smell and raw destructive power of our class.

We haven't doctored these pages to make them look as though we've always been right, had the correct analysis, or predicted everything in advance of it happening. We're only human beings, not full time revolutionary zombies from the planet Trotskoid. The pieces you read were part of *Class War*'s day-to-day interventions in the struggle and they reflect the urgency and, sometimes the confusion, of those events.

Starting out as a one off with a 500 circulation produc-

ed by three people on a rainy day in a council house in Mayhill, Swansea to fuck up the dead weight of pacifism and lack of class politics in the anarchist movement, the paper took off, struck a raw nerve. We didn't run away from the ferocity of our politics, deny or apologize for them as soon as we were confronted. We were fighting a class war for fuck's sake . . . no point having one hand tied behind your back. By any means necessary, as the man said. If a startled media rubbished us as brutal, nasty, violent, we said . . . GET USED TO IT, THERE'S LOTS MORE COMING YOUR WAY!

The decade ended as it began with riots in the streets of Oxford, Cardiff, Handsworth and Tyneside. During the 1980s, and now in the '90s, the British working class has refused to be cowed into submission – the past decade has been one of disorder not defeat. Now that the opposition and government have fused into one soggy moderate centre ground the time has come for us to move away from the margins, for our class to reassert its role as the driving force of our own destiny. That destiny is working class power. Now our disorder will become our power. Our time has come!

Cartoon accompaniment
from 'Breaking Free' by
J.Daniels. Available from
Attack International,Box
BM 6577,London WC1 3XX

WE HAVE FOUND NEW
HOMES FOR THE RICH

Rich Bastards BEWARE

OUR TIME HAS COME

While we're being fucked over every minute of our lives the rich bastards who are doing it are swanking it up all around us. Their life-styles are so different from ours that they might as well be from another fuckin planet. Just look at the Tatler or Harpers & Queen and see them planning their social year . . .

All this goes on under our fuckin noses, in the same world we live in, side by side with our everyday life. Yet these bastards get away with it scot free . . . with no aggravation towards them at all. It's like there's an invisible mental barrier which stops us going on the attack and restricts us to purely defensive actions, responding to their attacks.

WELL THESE BAD OLD DAYS ARE GOING TO END . . . We need to get in amongst these bastards. No more fuckin about on stupid Leftie marches for us. No more "Maggie, Maggie, Maggie . . . Out, out, out"'s. No more "What do we want . . . when do we want it"'s. No more "We demand this, we demand that" bollocks. No more "Save the GLC, solidarity with Nicaragua, stop the missiles" crap. No more "Blah, blah, blah, bleat,

bleat, bleat"'s. This kind of shit politics is for those whose opposition to the system is merely a hobby. We don't need special events to work up enthusiasm for a jolly good demo, eh what old chap! Our enemy is all around us everyday of our lives – all we've got to do is start putting the shits up the bastards.

At all events on the social calendars of the rich they expect to be left in tranquillity to enjoy themselves. We're supposed to suffer in silence, know our places, keep well away from them. After all that's what they give us beer, bingo and the Sun for.

BUT HERE'S SOME NEWS FOR YOU SCUMBAGS . . . FROM NOW ON THESE EVENTS AREN'T GOING TO BE INVITATION ONLY . . . WE'RE COMING TOO!!

CLASS WAR

MAY   20p

WE Must DEVASTATE the avenues WHERE the wealthy Live !'

LUCY PARSONS - 1885.

Hooray Henley

You are cordially invited to attend the

Henley Regatta

on Saturday JULY 6th

AT HENLEY ON THAMES, OXON.

M4 junction 8/9

....

ADMIT ONE TO THE ROYAL ENCLOSURE
(DRESS-BALACLAVA AND DMs!)

As a chauffeur serves champagne at a garden party in Millionaires row, Hampstead.

The first glimmers of fear flit across the faces of the rich as the rising tide of class anger rattles at their front gate.

Travelling down to Henley on a train full of Hooray Henrys pratting on about skiing in Switzerland and Lady Camilla's coming-out ball. How I managed to keep my gob shut and my hands from strangling the bastards is the 8th wonder of the world! This year there's a new topic of conversation though – the anarchists! Hooray Henriettas are assured by the Hooray Henrys that there'll be over a thousand police, some of them armed, there to protect them. They (but not me!) are reassured by the sight of a police helicopter and a hundred fat porkers sweltering in the sun in a school field just outside Henley. At Ealing Broadway 20 kids, many of them black, dive on to the train jeering the rich snobs and shoving them out the way. The considerable anxiety in the next carriage is further increased by the arrival of 10 casuals from Southall, well armed with Special Brew, and seemingly not going to Henley to watch the rowing.

Arrive at Henley station. Fuckin' hell, there's old bill everywhere! With our crafty disguises we slip through the police cordon but anyone not looking like an obvious rich bastard is turned back. The black kids don't make it off the platform. On every street corner there's a van load of pigs. By the bridge to the royal enclosure there's a control van, a breakdown vehicle to remove any motors blocking the bridge, and van-loads of back-up police. Police on the bridge are filtering people across, stopping anyone they don't like the look of. By now we've clocked a lot of class warriors from around the country blending in to the background – or at least trying to! Some Welsh hooligans have spent the night on posh boats on the Thames and have a few souvenirs to take home. We dive into the nearest boozer – all the pubs have security on the doors to keep out potential trouble-makers, but we manage to sneak through. More news comes through – there's riot police at the back of the police station and van-load after van-load of pigs.

After a few pints it's back onto the streets, a lot of punks have somehow got through. Let battle commence – we start harassing the stuck-up toffs on the streets. Stand in their way, trip them up, spit on them, abuse them, open well-shook-up cans of lager as they pass by in their hundreds of pounds dresses. Knock their boaters off, smash their sunglasses, kick the bastards.

They start to look really scared – despite the fact that there's a thousand police on duty they still can't be protected. Others are walking along the river bank kicking over hampers and champagne buckets; there's no resistance, they look petrified. Gradually a sizeable mob is assembling near the bridge – about 200 of us. We give up the low profile and stand hurling abuse, spit and the odd can and bottle at the rich. The Hoorays stop coming down the road. The police seal off the bridge, more pigs come running down the road, we're surrounded. We keep up the abuse for about 25 minutes. The police are getting fed up as we get into the second rendition of "Harry Roberts is our friend", very soon they're going to move in and nick the lot of us. Time to move on and resume guerrilla warfare. We filter away in 2's and 3's – there is no mass arrest: back to the guerrilla harassment of the bastards. We maraud all over the town. A BMW is turned over, the Tory Club window goes in, fists fly and some Hoorays decide to sunbathe fully clothed on the streets. Bricks and bottles fly over the back lanes into the gardens of rich mansions and startled sunbathers flee inside. Now a mercedes has gone over, all its windows caving in, posh cars are booted as their drivers try to speed past us down the road, pig vans are racing around trying to keep up with the action, there are some arrests. This goes on for a couple of hours till we gradully leave Henley. A trainload of Hoorays are plastered with their own strawberries as they leave, soaked in beer and anything else that comes to hand, their boaters and sunglasses end up on the tracks. They wish they'd never boarded this train to leave Henley but many rich bastards after Saturday wish they'd never gone there in the first place.

For the first time ever the rich have had to have over a thousand police, with helicopters, riot shields and armed units to protect them at one of their major social occasions. Many businesses, including garages and posh shops, closed down for the weekend preferring to lose their expected large profits rather than risk being smashed up. The rich now know what it's like to be under siege conditions, to be scared shitless everytime they wandered more than a few hundred yards from a policeman. The police are there to protect the rich and their wealth from the rest of us – well, from now on they're going to have to work a lot harder at it. This year there were a few hundred of us at Henley but next year there'll be thousands and the police will have to turn the place into a virtual prison for the rich to stop us getting at them.

The police are trying to make places where the rich are at their leisure, or where they live, no-go areas for working class people. At Wilmslow in Cheshire the Chief Inspector has said that black people from Moss Side will be arrested if they go there since their only reasons for being there can be to burgle the rich houses. At Henley black kids and anyone who didn't look posh enough were denied entry to the town or harassed or arrested by the police. We will continue to take our fight in to the streets of the rich ghettoes. There will be no no-go areas for us but we must make sure that working class areas become no-go areas for the rich – where they fear for their safety whenever they enter. We must continue to make them live under siege conditions.

Of course our sophisticated, intellectual revolutionary friends on the left will continue to deride us. From their well paid jobs as lecturers, social workers, probation officers and teachers propping up the system they allegedly despise, they will laugh patronisingly when we talk of jostling the rich in the streets. In Hampstead and Islington these wankers will prattle on about Nicaragua, Marxism today, yesterday and every fucking way. Cosily insulated from the rising class anger on the streets, for them politics is a trendy hobby. For us class hatred is a daily reality and one these wankers will find out about soon enough.

Henley is only part of our fight to build a working class movement designed to get rid of the rich and the police and politicians who protect them, once and for all.

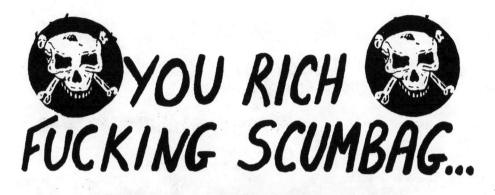 YOU RICH
FUCKING SCUMBAG...

WE'RE GONNA GET YOU.

JOIN THE CLASS WAR SPRING OFFENSIVE AGAINST THE RICH

★ ★ Class War's HOROSCOPE

Taurus (the Bull.)
Remember what bulls do to
china shops? We do the same
to snobby yuppy bistros.
Ole!

Gemini (the Twits.)
Forget the coming year--
you probably won't see any
of it. Better jump off an
office block while you still
have an office.

Cancer (the Crab.)
You'll make a lot of money
this year, but if you don't
share it out you could end
up dead.

Scorpio (the Scorpion.)
This would be a good year to
fuck off and die.

Sagittarius (the Windsor.)
Things are really falling
off at the moment - you're
almost totally snowed under.
A trip to a remote place
would be a good idea --
Especially if it's one way!

Capricorn (the Goat.)
Others will dig in their
heels and refuse to play
your game. A wrangle over
money matters in the coming
year could lead to you
getting lynched.

Leo (the Liar)
You really are a bastard!
Whatever happens to you
you'll be lucky to survive.

Fergo (the Parasite.)
A potentially good year for
you but unfortunately there
is no longer any room for
your class.

Libra (the Liberal.)
A wishy-washy year for you,
with some serious injuries
later on if you don't sort
out your politics.

**Aquarius (the water Petrol
Carrier.)**
Things will be looking hot for
for you this summer. Height
of fashion will be a burning
tyre around your neck.

Pisces (the Fish.)
You'll be seeing plenty of
these in the coming year
as you stand tall in your
concrete D.M.s and take
another breath of seawater.

Aries (the Ram.)
Others could be fed up
being treated like sheep.
Looks like being a bad year
for your volvo. Also your
head. Suggest you start
running

for Rich Bastards !★ ★

OLIVIA CHANNON MEMORIAL POSTER

step 1: lurk

BASH THE RICH

Three steps to Heaven

step 2: strike

step 3: leggit

In the long tradition of anonymous letter writing by the working class to the ruling class which goes back to the Luddites, the following 'welcome letter' to incoming rich homeowners has been circulating in Hackney, East London.

Dear Carpetbagger;

For some reason you have chosen to move to Hackney. It should be pointed out to you that this may be a grave mistake. While you live in your parasitic way of life, you are pushing up the cost of living for those of us who have lived here all our lives. We cannot afford the astronomical prices that you can.

THINK AGAIN! You are not wanted here and you serve no possible use to our community. It is very advisable that you sell up and go before house prices hit rock-bottom when the popularity of the area drops as a result of local hostility to you and your kind.

GO BACK WHERE YOU CAME FROM!

A YUPPIE ON THE STOCK EXCHANGE DEMONSTRATES HIS CURRENT LEVEL OF OPTIMISM....

FILO-FUCKED!

Why We Hate YUPPIES

Hackney

BMW's, Mercedes, Porsches — flash cars of every description have started to appear in the streets around where we live, parked in between the knackered old cortinas and escorts. Has everyone won the pools? No, its the parasitic YUPPIES moving in, trying to squeeze out the working class, pushing us out of the area — and they use their cars and their stupid status symbols to rub our noses in it.

JEALOUS

And when we smash up their cars or give them a bit of a kicking they always bleat "Jealousy!" Jealous? We're just ANGRY, it's pure class HATRED — because we know how they manage to live like they do in the midst of our hard times — and smashing their cars really hurts them. "Jealousy," they whine when their cosy little lives get shattered by a bit of FIGHTBACK. Every time I see one of their fucking posh cars it makes me realise that people like me will never get to live in a decent house, even though I work my arse off every day, because of greedy scum like them. There's enough money in the world, enough resources, enough houses for everyone to have what they need. But because the yuppies and the rest of the rich take a thousand times their share for doing sod all, except spending all day chatting away on their car phones about share prices to some prat in New York, it keeps us from getting the WEALTH WE CREATE and THEY SPEND.

It's a question of control, the rich control every part of our lives at the moment. Whether we're at work or on the dole, even where we live, everywhere. They affect us in different ways in different places though. In a lot of cities like London, Liverpool, Cardiff etc, it's the yuppies and the Urban Development Corporations who are coming to the area and breaking up working class communities, putting house prices up so that locals are driven out. They use their deadly wine bars and posh housing developments, to make us feel unwelcome in our own areas, and they even bulldoze council estates to make the view better. The sooner we make these bastards fuck off out of our areas the better.

YUPPIE Invasion

String 'em up

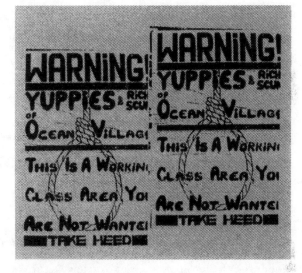

Whatever's happening elsewhere in the East End at the moment, there's no doubt that the Front Line in the class war against the Yuppie Invasion is on the Isle of Dogs.

As if the Canary Wharf development and the Docklands Light Railway weren't enough, working class people on the Island have to put up with watching hundreds of "ok yah" yuppies flooding into the quarter-of-a-million-pound-a-piece luxury homes that have been built only yards away from their rundown council blocks.

The LDDC, the press, the Police and the estate agents all try to give the impression that all is calm and peaceful — as the old East End fades quietly away in the sunset a wonderful new playground for the rich takes its place.

But the reality is completely different!

Class war is already raging on the Isle of Dogs.

BMWs are regularly broken into or nicked; new luxury homes are stripped bare of their appliances before and after the snobs move in, and "taxing the rich" in the form of Yuppie Mugging is fast becoming a bigger growth industry than Canary Wharf!

The new luxury estates with their built-in, over-the-top security protection, and the fear of a smack in the gob in the local boozer or of being "taxed" in the street, are making the yuppies virtual prisoners in their own homes!

Despite the estate agents' prattle, there's no warm East End welcome for these tossers.

The local youngsters, as they ease their own cash-flow problems, know that the days of petitions, Peoples' Armadas to parliament, and passive protests beloved of the Labour Party and community "leaders" have achieved sod all.

The Yuppie Invasion will only be stopped when they're too scared to move in, and those that're already here join the panic stampede to get back to their Surrey golf courses and Hampstead mansions.

Take our advice — Stay off the Isle of Dogs.

8 WAYS TO KEEP VERMIN LIKE THIS OUT OF YOUR VILLAGE

Pissed off with the Yuppie invasion of your village? Well here's how to get rid of them!

1. Ring the Church bells at 4.30 in the morning, every morning!

2. Let your goat into their prize rose garden, when they're off commuting to the office. By the time they come home it should look a treat!

3. Get your friendly farmer to drive his muck-spreader (switched on of course) past their open topped yuppie-mobile.

4. Organise a spot of rural rioting, with them as target number one!

5. Kidnap their snotty kids (on their way back from the local posh school) and leave them tied up in a cess-pit that hasn't been emptied since VE night!

6. Bring back the ancient village tradition of the ducking stool! If they float, burn them; if they don't, well it's saved you the job!

7. With petrol prices what they are, why don't you round 'em all up, harness them, and tow your tractor around the fields with them!

8. If the Church bells ain't enough for them, get the local morris dancers to practise outside their house every Sunday morning.

There you have it, a step-by-step guide to removing unwanted vermin from your village. Why not drop us a line and tell us how you got on, you never know, it might even make the next issue of your sizzling hot CLASS WAR.

Is Your Neighbour A YUPPIE?

All over Britain working class communities are being invaded by a plague of Yuppies. Now CLASS WAR introduces an exciting new quiz game to help you discover . . .

ARE THERE YUPPIES IN YOUR STREET?

All you have to do is pick one of the three answers for each of the eight questions (a, b or c). Keep a list of which answers you choose . . .

1. DO YOU LIVE NEAR . . .
(a) a disused dock or other expanse of water,
(b) a nice bit of open parkland or forest,
(c) a nuclear waste dump

2. DO YOUR NEIGHBOURS OWN . . .
(a) a brand new Porsche,
(b) a Cortina,
(c) a Citroen 2CV with a "Nuclear Power No Thanks" sticker on the back.

3. IF YOU WERE KNOCKED DOWN OUTSIDE YOUR HOUSE WOULD YOUR NEIGHBOURS . . .
(a) ring 999,
(b) get the brakes on their Citroen fixed,
(c) negotiate with your kids to buy your house for £¼ million.

4. WHEN YOUR NEIGHBOURS COME ROUND TO BORROW SOMETHING IS IT USUALLY . . .
(a) a cup of sugar,
(b) Nescafe 'Gold Blend' coffee,
(c) your butler.

5. DOES YOUR NEIGHBOUR'S BACK GARDEN . . .
(a) back on to a railway siding,
(b) contain a ready-made barbeque unit,
(c) my neighbours have no garden, they have a yacht mooring instead.

6. NEW NEIGHBOURS MOVE IN NEXT DOOR. DO THEY . . .
(a) invite you round for a cup of tea,
(b) invite you round for cocktails,
(c) invite their friends round and show you to them as an example of local culture.

7. WHEN YOUR NEIGHBOURS GO ON HOLIDAY DO THEY ASK YOU TO . . .
(a) look after their dog,
(b) watch out for burglars,
(c) check that the security guards they've hired are doing their jobs.

8. DO YOUR NEIGHBOURS READ . . .
(a) Financial Times, Telegraph, Investors Monthly,
(b) The Guardian, Independent, Socialist Worker,
(c) Daily Mirror, Class War.

	a	b	c
1	10	5	0
2	10	0	5
3	0	5	10
4	0	5	10
5	0	5	10
6	0	5	10
7	0	5	10
8	10	5	0

The points for each of the answers you've chosen are shown in the table opposite.

Now add up your score and see how well you did . . .

0-25: Doesn't look like there's any yuppies about at the moment. However, you're probably fed up with other things like street crime or bad housing. *Remedy*: set up a Class War group and do something about it!

25-65: Not a full scale yuppie invasion . . . yet. But it looks like you've got a few of the 'advance guard' . . . the trendy lefties! They're probably taking over your local council so be prepared. *Remedy*: get your Class War group organised quickly. You haven't got much time left!

66-79: Looks like you've had it. The yuppies are well and truly here. Be prepared to get an eviction notice any day. You obviously left it too late to set up your Class War group: *Remedy*: Burn their filofaxes!

80 POINTS: to score this high you must be a bleedin' yuppie yourself, and if so what're you doing reading this book?! *Remedy*: Please send us your name and address and we'll make sure you get your next instalment of Class War delivered personally!

CHARLES HAVING A PHILOSOPHICAL CONVERSATION WITH
'MILDRED' THE YUKKA AT THE ROYAL FANCY DRESS BALL!

The Royals

WHO GIVES a toss if the Royal parasites in the shape of Fergie and Di aren't going to have any more kids?

The media responded to this excellent news in their usual slavish way by trotting out hordes of so-called "royal experts" to spout on about the subject.

Myself, I think we'd all be better off with no more Royals at all, *have all the males sterilised*, that would stop the in-breeding bastards dropping any more sprogs for us to keep in a life of idle luxury.

Anyhow, I couldn't see Fergie having any more kids, it would get in the way of all her skiing trips and shopping expeditions.

And Prince Charles seems to prefer the company of loony philosophers and talking plants to his wife, *so more kids seem unlikely for them also!*

HATED

Whilst we're on the subject, the only good thing I've read about Royalty recently is that most people hate them!

Their shopping, holiday and leisure excursions, whilst a war rages in the Gulf, have got right up the noses of ordinary people.

Most Hated Royalty No 1 comes in as no surprise — FERGIE; the parasite we all love to loathe. This blustering, big headed, money-grabbing, over the top Sloane Ranger has had more holidays than Thomas Cook!

And she twists the knife in the back of most women by whinging and moaning about how difficult it is to raise two children with "only" three nannies, fifteen servants and being a member of one of the richest families of the world!

The Royals are immensely rich, powerful, pampered and privileged, all that they have to concern them is which chic ski resort, fashionable London restaurant, top notch Polo match or exclusive Caribbean island will they go to next.

They are not special, different, dedicated, but spoilt and self indulgent. How much longer will we tolerate their excesses?

another fucking royal
PARASITE

ROYAL EXCLUSIVE!

IS THIS THE REAL QUEEN ?

CLASS WAR REVEALS SENSATIONAL ROYAL COVER UP –

Real Queen LOCKED UP

THE REAL
KATHERINE BOWES-LYON

On 6th April it was revealed that the Queen's cousin, Katherine Bowes-Lyon, had been shut away in a mental hospital for the last 46 years. NOW CLASS WAR CAN REVEAL NEWS EVEN MORE SHOCKING THAN THAT. News which NONE of the Fleet Street press dare print and which has been hidden from history by one of the biggest cover-ups by the establishment of this or any other century!

That poor woman, ALLEGEDLY Katherine Bowes-Lyon, is in fact Elizabeth, daughter of King George VI and the Queen Mother – AND THE RIGHTFUL QUEEN OF ENGLAND!

COVER-UP

It is the *true Queen herself* who has been shut away in a mental hospital while the real Katherine Bowes-Lyon has masqueraded in her place as Queen Elizabeth. Neither woman knows the truth and, indeed, it is only the Queen Mother alive today who does, since it involved a conspiracy of silence at the heart of the Royal Family, stretching back over 60 years! That conspiracy was to hide from the British people that strong strain of madness which permeated the British Royals. *What other explanation can there be for the horrific treatment of this poor mentally handicapped woman?*

On April 21st 1926 a first baby was born to the future King George VI and Elizabeth Bowes-Lyon, now the Queen Mother. It is this baby that is now the rightful Queen Elizabeth. But it was spotted at once that she was severely mentally handicapped. Although this occurred nine years before the abdication crisis of 1936 which was to see this baby's father unexpectedly become King

George VI, it was felt too dangerous to allow it to be known that the case of madness had struck so close to the potential successor to the crown.

The Queen Mother's brother, John Bowes-Lyon, and his wife Fenella Bowes-Lyon were expecting the birth of another child only two months after the birth of the mentally handicapped Elizabeth. She was born Katherine Bowes-Lyon, a normal healthy baby, on July 4th 1926 – less than ten weeks after Elizabeth!!

In the greatest possible secrecy, known only to the parents of both girls themselves and the future King's personal surgeon, the girls were swapped by their families – the healthy Katherine Bowes-Lyon taking on the future identity of Queen Elizabeth and the true Elizabeth living with her aunt and uncle as Katherine Bowes-Lyon. Both girls were protected from the public eye in the early years so that the ten week age discrepancy became unnoticeable.

With George's accession to the throne, the phoney Elizabeth became first in line for the succession and it became even more important that the secret never got out. In 1941, at the height of the war, the girl now known as Katherine Bowes-Lyon was secretly admitted to the Surrey mental hospital where she has remained hidden ever since. The process of her disappearance was completed when all mention of her mysteriously vanished from Debrett's and she was listed as having died in 1961 in Burke's Peerage.

We believe that it must have been the *Queen Mother herself* who furnished this false information, unknown to other members of the Windsor and Bowes-Lyon families. In this way she would have been able to erase the memory of her true daughter from her mind, and remove the necessity for any visits which may have aroused suspicions.

The major question is: Why the cover up?

WINDSOR CURSE

CLASS WAR can now reveal that for generations the Royal Family has been plagued by mental illness – known as the *Windsor Curse*.

● The Queen's demented great uncle, the Duke of Clarence, was extremely violent and was widely suspected of being *Jack the Ripper*, the maniac who murdered prostitutes in the 19th century. The eldest son of King Edward VII, he was destined to be king himself until he suddenly – and quite conveniently – died of pneumonia.

● Another ancestor, King George III, suffered from an inherited blood disease causing mental disturbance, and he became known as the "Mad Monarch".

● In more recent times, Prince John, the younger brother of the Queen Mother's husband, was shut away at Sandringham all his life – separated from his healthy brothers and sisters – to hide him from the world. The truth has never been told about him but it has many parallels with what has happened to Katherine Bowes-Lyon.

● Tatiana Mountbatten – niece of Prince Charles' late uncle Lord Mountbatten – is an extremely violent patient secretly locked away in a Northampton mental hospital.

ROYAL HORROR!

HOWEVER, the most sensational case of all was the hideous being locked away in Glamis Castle – the Queen Mother's home – for over one hundred years, and directly related to the Queen and other royals. He was born a monster and lived for 100 years hidden from view in a secret room in the thick walls of the castle. At night he was exercised on the roof. The secret was *covered up* by an entry in Debrett's Peerage of 1841 claiming that he had died at birth! Sounds familiar doesn't it? He was mentally handicapped and developed a massive body, covered in thick black hair. He was said to have been egg-

CLASS WAR
SAYS.....

ROYAL FASHION

Original engraving of the horror
of Glamis Castle by the pensioned
off slater in Australia.

TURN ON
THE CARBONMONOXIDE!

This necklace, a gift
from the People !

shaped, with tiny legs and arms, and a head sunk deep in the vast barrel of his chest. Once, he was spotted in his cell by a slater making roof repairs. The terrified man was sworn to secrecy, given a pension and sent off to Australia. The "Horror of Glamis Castle" is believed to have still been there when the Queen Mother was brought up as a child in the early part of this century – so the practice of locking away unfortunate relatives would have been familiar to her.

CHARLES FEAR

Their great fear is that this strain of madness is now showing itself in the future king, Prince Charles; he talks to plants, dabbles with the occult, and wanders around alone in the Kalahari Desert. It is said that the Queen Mother will never allow her "daughter" to abdicate for fear of Charles' incipient lunacy!

WHY WE HAVE EXPOSED THIS?

Politically we are opposed to the wealthy parasites of the Royal Family. They sponge off the backs of the work-

ing class while claiming to be great upholders of morality. We take no pleasure in revealing their mental illness – normally we would think it irrelevant to our class politics. After all, our allegedly "sane" world leaders cause far more mayhem than any mentally ill Royal.

But the madness of the Royals has been covered up for centuries for fear that the monarchy would collapse if the public knew the truth.

Now we have exposed what could be the cover-up of the century. The public know that the Royal family numbers amongst them the suspected Jack the Ripper, a demented one hundred year old "egg", and countless others secretly locked away in mental hospitals. The few "sane" ones are, it would appear from this terrible tale, engaged in lying and deceit to protect their privileged position.

May the thieving, scheming Windsor family rot in hell and the mentally ill ones still alive be treated as ordinary human beings with the compassion they deserve, rather than being locked up for years so the others can prosper.

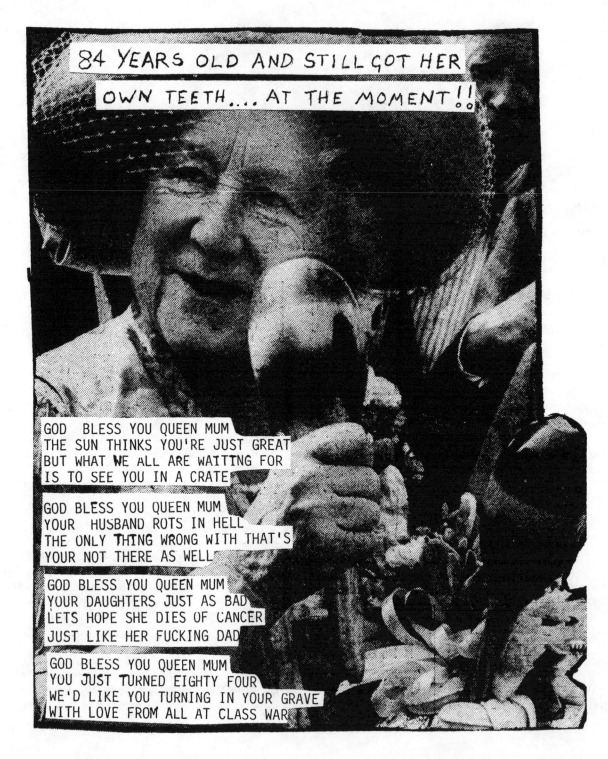

84 YEARS OLD AND STILL GOT HER
OWN TEETH... AT THE MOMENT!!

GOD BLESS YOU QUEEN MUM
THE SUN THINKS YOU'RE JUST GREAT
BUT WHAT WE ALL ARE WAITING FOR
IS TO SEE YOU IN A CRATE

GOD BLESS YOU QUEEN MUM
YOUR HUSBAND ROTS IN HELL
THE ONLY THING WRONG WITH THAT'S
YOUR NOT THERE AS WELL

GOD BLESS YOU QUEEN MUM
YOUR DAUGHTERS JUST AS BAD
LETS HOPE SHE DIES OF CANCER
JUST LIKE HER FUCKING DAD

GOD BLESS YOU QUEEN MUM
YOU JUST TURNED EIGHTY FOUR
WE'D LIKE YOU TURNING IN YOUR GRAVE
WITH LOVE FROM ALL AT CLASS WAR

YET ANOTHER PICTURE OF THE QUEEN MUM LOOKING GOOD. SUPRISE SUPRISE. THIS ALKIE OLD FAG HAG AIN'T HAD TO SCRUB NO FLOORS NEITHER.

AUSTRALIAN MOTHER CLAIMS DINGO TOOK BABY

Lindy Chamberlain, accused of the killing of ... ... in the Ayer's ro...

WHERE WERE THE DINGOS WHEN WE REALLY NEEDED THEM?

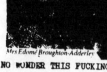

Mrs Edome Broughton-Adderley

NO WONDER THIS FUCKING OLD COW DOESN'T SHOW HER AGE. SHE HASN'T DONE A STROKE IN HER LIFE.

NO GOOD LOOKING JEALOUS KOO. THIS LOOK TAKES YEARS OF POVERTY AND CHILDCARE TO ACHEIVE.

THIS LOOK IS PARTICULARLY POPULAR WITH LADIES WHO COMBINE NIGHTSHIFT WITH AN EARLY MORNING CLEANING JOB AND AT LEAST SIX HOURS HEAVY HOUSEWORK. ONLY THE TRULY DETERMINED GO FOR THIS 'FULL OF CHARACTER' LOOK.

HOW TOTALLY AMAZING. THIS LADY IS 40 AND LOOKS 60. SHE MUST HAVE LED AN EXTRAORDINARILY FULL AND ACTIVE LIFE.

THIS BINT WOULDN'T LIFT A FINGER TO HELP HELP ANYONE BUT HERSELF.

FERGIE FOALS AGAIN!
   THE BAD NEWS IS OUT! OVER-FED FERGIE IS EXPECTING ANOTHER LITTLE PARASITE TO ADD TO THE GROWING ROYAL COLLECTION!
   I only hope that bothmother and baby die in childbirth, and the rest of the Royal brood go with them !

BETTER DEAD
THAN WED

Queen's Father Was Hitler SHOCK

'MICHAEL'- WHAT A STUPID
FUCKING NÂME FOR A PRINCESS !

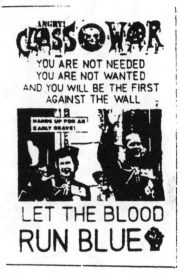

So Princess Michael's dad was a nazi. Look at the family she married into! They've been the elite of a ruling class that has been massacring and murdering people for centuries. And they will continue to do so, unless we stop them. Behind the smiling faces of the royals lies a squalid world where human life is bartered for an extra percentage of profit. The elite swan around showing off their baubles while faceless drones tot up their bank balances. What does it matter if these scum dress up in swastikas or not? They are tooled up with nuclear weapons that can murder 6 million people in a few seconds.

While we are faced with this situation we have the papers telling us to celebrate VE Day, the final victory over nazism. They must be joking. It was not our victory. It was a victory for King and Country, a bosses' victory. They can celebrate because they know that millions of working class people died for them. Now they expect us to turn on the telly and watch them living for us. Sometimes it's the spectacle of a royal wedding or a royal

baby. Other times it's the fictional world of Dallas.

Our victory will be totally different. We will not win fighting under the flag of democracy, letting silver-tongued politicians and smooth-operating industrialists build their empires over our dead bodies. We will fight as an independent and autonomous class. We will not accept the authority of any boss class, not even if it emerges from our own ranks. We will not accept the logic of capitalism which always places personal gain over being part of a living community.

We've seen this fight in the miners strike. We see it everyday in our own lives in much smaller ways: kids refusing to grass up their mates to teachers, workers covering for each other while they skive, etc.

Our struggle is not advanced by working out abstract political platforms, but by expanding the ways we stick by one another, by making our social worlds stronger and better able to resist the carrot of being bought off, or the stick of repression. Only when we are able to wield our own power will our opinions be worth a toss.

Running RIOTS

COMMUNITY COP CLOBBERING

The best Saturday night out for four years – bleeding brilliant – sheer inspiration – fucking WONDERFUL! We took on the murdering fascist pigs as a community on our own turf, and smashed them. The people of the whole area were on the streets confronting the cops – burning cars, blocking roads, bricks and petrol bombs for Brixton nick, Bill bastards running, shitting themselves. What a pity it doesn't happen in rich areas like Hampstead . . . Well, the Brixton explosion did spread out into Clapham, Streatham, Dulwich and Peckham – a good sign that people are beginning to realise that the pickings are richer in such areas. Everyone was out the next day trying out their new cameras and ghetto blasters! The Press slither back into the area they were beaten up and thrown out of the night before. They spew out their usual fucking Kak about "unemployment" and "deprivation", whilst pissing it up with putrid local politicians and Uncle Tom "community leaders" dining on their own words – only last week everyone was congratulating themselves that the absence of riots after Handsworth and Toxteth was all because of "how wonderful Lambeth Council is" and "how the community love the cops really" and "it's all the fault of a few extremists" – Kak Kak Kak . . . The community was out on the streets on Saturday night because the Inspector ▓▓▓▓▓▓▓ Lovelock shot a black mother of six and put her in a wheelchair for life. If it hadn't been her it could have been her 22 year old son – only he'd be *dead*. The result of this was a spontaneous explosion of class rage – of community hatred against the ▓▓▓ incompetent, ▓▓▓ action of Inspector ▓▓▓▓▓ Lovelock – a so-called fucking "Firearm Expert" – and his ▓▓▓▓▓ friends – the Community Police. All this is conveniently forgotten by his idiot boss the Chief Constable of Lambeth Commander Alec Marnoch who drivels on with mindfucking stupidity about "visiting agitators from Handsworth" – what a load of fucking bullshit! No, as EVERYONE knows the riots were started, organised and led by Communist Alien Stormtroops from the red planet Bolleaux, who

▓▓▓ Original version available from Class War

landed on the roof of the fucking Ritzy!!! When are the stupid pig shits going to wise up to the fact that we riot in response to the particularly vile acts of oppression by the *class enemy: the cops.* We fight these bastards with all our force and all our strength BECAUSE WE HATE THEM. The Police are the Class Traitors. They have always been, are now and will always be our Sworn Enemy.

Street JUSTICE

Once again the streets of Brixton have erupted following yet another police outrage, in this case the cowardly shooting of an unarmed black woman as they raided her house early on a Saturday morning. By six o'clock that evening angry local residents had surrounded Brixton police station, putting it in a virtual state of siege. The filth cowered inside as bricks rained down on the station. Only after it had been petrol bombed, as flames licked the paintwork and scaffolding did the police move out in large numbers protected by large riot shields. With this fighting spread rapidly until the area around the station, including Brixton Road, was a mass of burning barricades, constructed from hi-jacked cars. For the next six hours the police were tied down by a combination of set piece confrontations, mobs using hit and run tactics, and an outbreak of mass looting. Sunday afternoon saw more confrontations, as did the evening. Also sporadic clashes occured in other areas of South London.

Fortunately not only the police have learned from the lessons of '81. The rioters also used new methods to counter police advances. More burning cars to hold back the police, who when they suceed in breaking through, face an empty street and another blazing barricade. This time everyone wears masks to avoid identification. Rather than trying to hold indefensible positions once the police have become reinforced, the fighters hold the estates, making incursions against the filth, then

PHEW! WHAT A SCORCHER

retreating. Hit and run. Gone are the days when a mob held the "front line" bearing the brunt of police attacks.

Now the forces of "law and order" face local youth who know their estates backwards. Into these areas the police are reluctant to enter.

Equally important for us is the political awareness displayed by the fighters. The petrol bombing of a self proclaimed "community leader" as he appealed for calm outside the police station. The attack on the local Conservative club. In spite of lying press reports it was nothing like a "race riot" at all. The unity between black and white insurgents was far greater than in '81 (about half of those arrested were white). Many journalist toads were singled out for a well deserved kicking. Not the actions of a mindless "criminal" mob. This time only a total fool would drone on about "unemployment" and "the need for jobs". It's plain and obvious that a section of the working class has risen up against the whole idea of policing and the police . . . All cops were targets that weekend as they will continue to be. The die is cast.

Some reports from the more lurid papers talked about 14 year old "disco dollies" firebombing the police. The actions of these youngsters in Brixton Rd early on that Saturday evening are worth far more to our class than 100 resolutions passed at the pathetic Labour Party and TUC conferences. How ironic that as the gutless worms who delude themselves in to thinking they are our representatives debated at Blackpool, both Toxteth and Peckham erupted. Put simply these are the only choices for our class, falling for this bullshit about "kicking out the Tories" & "electing a Labour government" or insurrection on the streets. Never mind all this crap about waiting another 2 years for the next election, some of these kids can't wait another 2 weeks for the next flare up. It is only from these confrontations that revolutionary awareness will develop – where else is there for our class?

As for the looting, Labour might, along with the rest of the left, prattle on about the redistribution of wealth. The looters are actually practising it! Fuck all this shit about working class shops, there's no such thing, it's a contradiction of terms. Such things are inevitable in the

initial stages of rebellion. And it keeps the cops busy too. With the muggings it seems that the mood of many involved in the fighting was that you either took part alongside them against the police or left, "Fight or fuck off". And from their mood, it seemed there was little room for by-standers. The police had shot a woman, war had been declared. You were either with the fighters or not. If not you were fair game in their eyes. Even so, many attempted, and succeeded in, preventing muggings, even as the fighting raged.

And as for the conspiracy theories emanating from the wooden head of moron police commander Marnoch, that we in Class War were behind the riots, spreading rumours alongside other "outside" agitators, all we say is "bollocks". The people of Brixton don't need us to spark them off. We fully admit that many of us were there and took an active part in the proceedings. We don't have a "base" in Brixton. It may come as a shock to the forces of law and order, but only a handful of us actually live in the area. And fuck it – why shouldn't we pour into the riot area to fight alongside our comrades and our class?

(Besides we'd like to know, do all these riot police live in Brixton?)

Since, Brixton, Toxteth and Peckham have been the scenes of more anti-police confrontations, thus showing what lies ahead. Of course when fighting breaks out it is our duty to spread it and wear down the police. But rather than speculate about "what is to be done", "setting up workers' councils" etc etc, the only immediate logical step we see is the creation of "no-go" areas, from which the police and forces of government will be totally and permanently banned. No go areas will not be places where crime rules, it rules our streets already. We want riot to develop into uprising and insurrection. In no go areas the working class must exercise their class power, refusing to hand anything over to "leaders", "political", "community" or otherwise. Rather than an end in itself this will be the first major crack in the system. As I write this, according to the radio, police are under attack in Liverpool. This is not "protest". It's part of the working class flexing its muscle. The scene is set for the future!

Skull and cross bones. Symbol of peace and happiness.

BUY
CLASS WAR
OR FUCK OFF !

RICH
BAST
ARD

BE
WARE
!!!

WHOEVER THEY
VOTE FOR
WE ARE
UNGOVERNABLE

THE WORKING
CLASS STRIKES
BACK

On The RAMPAGE

STOP THE CITY

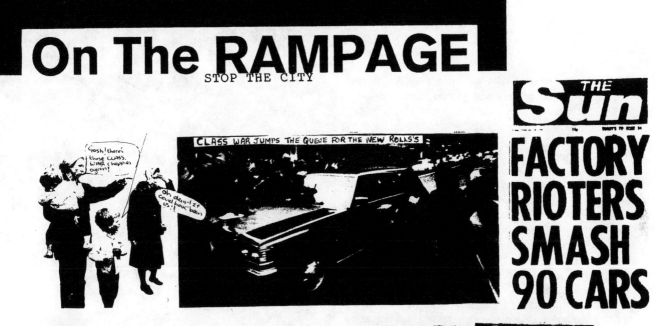

Speech bubble: "Gosh! there's those CLASS WAR chappies again!"

Speech bubble: "Oh dear! It could have been us!"

Caption: CLASS WAR JUMPS THE QUEUE FOR THE NEW ROLLS'S

THE Sun

FACTORY RIOTERS SMASH 90 CARS

Wild in the city

Stop the City was fuckin brilliant. What a change from last time. Cars overturned; a Bentley completely trashed; loads of plate glass windows in banks and finance houses smashed with bricks, dustbins and bus stops; tyres slashed; rich bastards glued up inside their own cars; spray paint graffiti everywhere; fuckin huge orange smoke canisters choking up the whole street; the police covered in red paint from the paint bombs among the bottles, fruit and rubbish hurled at them; rich brat stockbrokers jostled and gobbed on; a cop fleeing into a wine bar before being smacked in the face; collective shop-lifting as girlie mags and beauty products were dumped in the street and set on fire among the already smouldering waste bins and skips and fur coats. Organised shoves and charges at the police to bust our way out of the Royal Exchange; people pulled back and rescued from the cops. Best of all the collective rampages away from the Royal Exchange – enforcing our power on the rich for a change. As they skulked fearfully behind the windows of their brokers' offices and banks we were in control of the streets rather than the police they looked for in vain to protect them and their property. A lorryload of bricks is gleefully discovered and its contents redistributed through plate glass windows all down Fenchurch Street. We run round the corner, half expecting to see the old bill, but only to meet another anarchist mob coming the other way. We leap in the air and greet each other like quarrymen meeting up as they tunnel through the Alps!

Most of the arrests take place round the Royal Exchange but when we get mobile the police can't keep up. Small groups go their own way, meet up for the maximum damage large scale rampages, melt away and reform again. Despite the arrests *the police are beaten – we've fucking won!* When we're confined to one area with one target in one static group we've got no chance but STC shows that when we're mobile, not confined to one target and willing to put ourselves about then we can keep on winning.

STC has shown that we've now got an anarchist movement in Britain . . . a movement that can organise effective initiatives on its own, pull thousands onto the streets, and is at last willing to take violent action. Less than a year ago 700 people were still getting nicked for doing fuck all, sitting on their arses at Upper Heyford. Last September 200 people were still getting nicked for doing sod all at the first STC. But changes were taking place. The uselessness of pacifism was increasingly obvious as holding hands and die-ins achieved fuck all. Meanwhile the Animal Liberation Front were mounting the most effective and successful direct action campaign for years. People who were smashing up property to rescue animals or trash butchers' shops were going to apply the lessons learned elsewhere. On the October 22nd CND march an effective anarchist mob of 300-400 fought with the police and tried to storm the stage. Now we've had STC with over 2,000 on the streets. People who were pacifists 6 months ago are now trashing shops and fighting the police. The whole atmosphere has completely changed – confidence and combativity are in the air rather than resignation and passivity.

Buildings blaze

Smashing Time

In comparison to the first 'Stop the City' the second protest on March 29th was like a breath of fresh air. Going far beyond the usual passive wanks so beloved of the Left and Greenpeace types, the physical damage to innumerable city institutions such as dozens of banks was tremendously uplifting for all involved. According to some of the more sensational daily newspapers... "Skinheads, homosexuals, punks, anarchists, animal liberationists and (believe it or not) Greenham women" had teamed up to smash bank windows, turn over Rolls Royces and frighten office workers. While we can't be sure about the latter, we certainly left more than a few calling cards with the former two. These amazing events were mostly spontaneous, for whenever groups broke free from the massive police presence surrounding the main meeting place at the Bank of England, they were able to rampage to their heart's content before the filth could rush reinforcements to the area. By which time people had wisely vanished, only to appear later, elsewhere to repeat the performance. No one group can claim responsibility for the damage that ensued, it being a product of all who participated.

ON THE RAMPAGE

We think that this momentum has to be maintained, increased even. Our movement in all its diversity requires a physical presence on the streets as the first tentative step towards creating situations that go beyond mere protest. There's a slight, but in our view desirable, possibility that the energy and willingness to go beyond the almost farcical first 'Stop the City' mentality, if allied to wider social disturbances, could be the beginning of a genuine autonomous youth movement. Such a current, if political and capable of developing imaginative ideas and tactics, could also spread into sections of the working class proper, with drastic consequences for the established order. Full encouragement and participaton is our attitude to this development.

On the negative side 400 arrests is totally unacceptable. In the numerous discussions and meetings that will be held in the wake, we must as of necessity try to develop tactics to ensure that this isn't repeated at future events. One arrest is one too many!

LAWLESS BRITAIN

There's a realisation by the majority of the participants that they come from marginal elements in society. True, but as has been illustrated throughout history, and recently abroad, this usually happens. We'll measure our ultimate success when we pull in those less marginalised such as the construction workers who cheered us on. Many of the people who work in the city may find themselves thrown on the scrapheap by a combination of the economic crisis and new technology over the next few years. It's imperative that they, the working class and the marginalised link up for an all out assault on the entire capitalist system. Already some of those who shared in the experience of Stop the City are stumbling towards this realisation. Let's hope they don't get diverted in their progress by leftism and all that shit.

the aggro goes on STOP THE CITY

The destructive actions on Stop the City – or should we say constructive actions – represent to us what a full-blooded anarchist movement should be. We have two choices, either we have a movement of middle class wankers like teachers, social workers, solicitor types, radical journalists and mindless pacifists that revolves around a cheese and wine circuit or a movement that takes to the streets, displays imagination and daring while opening up avenues of discussion so far confined to a tiny minority and explores new methods of relating to one another in everyday life with the goal of destroying the system for once and all. Simple as that.

NICK NACK PADDY WACK

thousands of chanting miners went to war on Parliament behind a hail of flying bottles, boots and fists.

The mob tried to storm the Palace of Westminster by swarming over security railings.

Terrified children and tourists ran for cover as the bloody battle spilled across Parliament Square, forcing nearby Westminster Bridge to be closed.

Mounted police broke up the demo as bottles and beer cans rained down, while MPs debated the pit strike in the Commons.

Miners in battle of Commons

GIVE A DOG A BONE
COPS ARE BATTERED

The Queen has been shocked by clashes between miners and the police, says OUR POLITICAL CORRESPONDENT. He quotes informed sources as saying that nothing has shocked her more since the inner city riots of 1981.

Her Majesty's right on the fucking ball here-the miners strike is the biggest threat to the state since the riots of 81. From Ollerton and Mansfield to the battles of Orgreave what we have now is far more than a strike. In areas like South Yorkshire whole communities are involved in an almost insurrectionary state of class war with the bosses and the police. Kids walk out of schools, women fight alongside men on the picket lines, at Maltoy the local police station is under siege every weekend and the cons can only patrol the streets in their hundreds with full riot gear support.

MANSFIELD
MALTBY
ORGREAVE
WHY AIN'T YOUR TOWN ON THE ROLL OF HONOUR?!

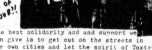

The best solidarity and and support we can give is to get out on the streets in our own cities and let the spirit of Toxteth '81 meet up with the spirit of Orgreave '84 Memo to: H.M. Elizabeth II-You ain't seen nothing yet ma'am !!

WHY DON'T THE OLD BILL

CLASS WAR
CONFERENCE
LONDON 27ᵀᴴ-29ᵀᴴ JULY
DETAILS FROM: BOX C.W. ALBANY ST. BOOKS 36 ALBANY ST. LONDON N.W.1.

...but where's the analysis?

POLICE broke up a gang of punks and skinheads who tried to disrupt the Rose Ball in London's Mayfair last night. The gang of 40, who claimed to be from the anarchy group Class War, had threatened to throw urine and tomatoes at guests as they arrived at the Grosvenor House Hotel in Park Lane. One punk said: "We hate the rich bastards."

FUCK OFF HOME!!

Open Up
The Second Front

On the terrain of industrial dispute we can claim, without the slightest fear of contradiction, that the miners' strike has gone far beyond anything seen on mainland Britain. No mere wage struggle this, with everything played according to the book (i.e. mostly non violent – excepting of course the police).

The positive aspects of this strike, which have on occasion erupted into brutal class war, are evident even for those of us who rely upon the sickening diet of newspapers and television for our misinformation.
So, what do we regard as positive?

Mass proletarian violence that has ranged from set-piece confrontations involving thousands of massed pickets and police. Not only the classic push and shove tussle, but full scale riots with intensive stone throwing, barricade building, wreckage and arson.

Violence not only at colliery gates and power plants, but police stations in pit villages attacked without warning, police and scab convoys ambushed, the birth of 'paramilitary' hit squads causing vast amounts of damage to NCB property. Cowboy outfits profiting from

strike-breaking and related activities have also been visited. Nothing within living memory has ever happened here on such an extensive scale. Not only have the police deployed riot equipment but such scenes have become commonplace. A precedent for the future?

The spirit of determination exhibited by the strikers, holding out against the massive police onslaught while showing no sign of caving in to pig intimidation.

Allied to this is the fact that the communities in solid areas are standing together with no intention of slinking back to work defeated. The strength of this struggle derives not only from the workplace but the community. (By community we don't mean the idealistic pipe-dream of some inner city lefty gentrification, but a vibrant living entity). The impressive involvement of women's support groups is a product of this.

As an added bonus, scattered reports and rumours, somewhat difficult to substantiate at the moment, have been percolating down to us that some groups of miners no longer care whether they return to work or not. Others, in spite of the obvious hardships, are enjoying the longest break in their working lives. The repossessed

Mob fights police

videos and tv sets haven't caused mass outbreaks of despair, contrary to expectations. Violent class conflict has temporarily freed a section of the working class from hollow consumerism. We've also heard that small groups of miners are beginning to show an interest in anarchist policies.

We don't see the miners as passive victims of police brutality. In the heat of class war many are indeed on the receiving end of police and truncheons but as far as we're concerned the more violence and injuries the miners inflict on the police the better.

However, the strikers have shown extraordinary signs of autonomous initiative, ignoring union pleas to keep it within limits that have crippled the working class.

Hit squads, attacks on police stations, incidents during mass pickets such as Orgreave, are an indication, a pointer to unknown territory. It's not the purpose of this article to 'criticise' Scargill and the NUM. Sufficient to say that we don't in any way regard the unions as revolutionary organisations. The time for post-mortems will be after any sell-out. But neither is it our task to berate other comrades for their rightful criticisms.

At this point we'd also like to mention some of the negative aspects of this struggle:

The striking miners are not questioning, so far, the nature of unionism, its role in capitalist society, the system. This probably won't happen until the final phase of the dispute, particularly if any sell-out or compromise is too blatant.

There's no denying that the police, in some areas, have constituted themselves into a virtual army of occupation, employing a terror so far only experienced by the rebellious young of the decaying inner cities.

The police have also had the chance to perfect the future strategy of state repression. Still, it's better the pigs suffer their casualties in a genuine struggle than in riot training. The strikers, not without cost (over 5,000 arrests) have also learnt a thing or two.

The ferocity of the struggle has tended to obscure a glaring fact. The miners stand alone. Below, we hope to indicate an untried path that could remedy this situation, drastic action that doesn't require the "assistance" of the TUC.

One of the most repellant aspects of the dispute has

THE MINERS HAD THE RIGHT IDEA
- -

A noose is dangled in front of Norman Willis
at a miners rally in Port Talbot

been the behaviour of the self-proclaimed leftist vanguards. Swooping like trained hawks they see the conflict in terms of paper sales and eventual recruitment. It goes without saying that the majority of these individuals are from a background far removed from that of the proletarian fraternity. Nevertheless the amount of demoralisation they are capable of causing is tremendous, perhaps more so in the wake of the strike. Even when performing what appear to be useful tasks such as collecting money "for the miners", rumours abound about misappropriation of cash raised, some of it apparently being hived off into party projects.

Even more revolting (if such things can be imagined) is the attitude of the TUC and Labour party, whose leaders are more concerned with preventing proletarian violence than winning the strike. Kinnock is even resorting to a form of left-nationalism in his pathetic attempts to curb the healthy development of class violence. It's "alien to the temperament and the intelligence of the British trade union movement". Nor will ballots. Instinctively, if nothing else, the strikers are aware of this, yet still they listen and tolerate Labour politicians prattling on about 'victory' at their rallies. Politically the strikers have yet to make the break. But that's not to say it won't happen.

Never mind the left, Labour Party and TUC. What has the anarchist contribution been? Collecting for the miners may ease the conscience of some anarchists. Sure, we all give money for good but really there isn't all that much difference between collecting for the strikers and the starving of Africa. Going to the picket lines makes no real overall difference. What's another couple of dozen here or there mean? Most of the anarchist papers do little but pour out irrelevances. A class war raging and one calls for a ballot! Others go to the other extreme and print articles offering full support – to the UM bureaucracy! Another idiot writes that the miners can be starved into revolution!

So, after 6 months of this momentous strike, with the prospect of it lasting into 1985, we seriously propose a state of minor insurgency as the real anarchist contribution.

In the past, we of the autonomist/class war type current have been ridiculed when we predicted mass political violence on the streets during the comparatively tranquil mid-70s. With the struggle against the Nazis, the foundations were laid for the uprisings of '81. Again we predicted this occurrence fairly accurately. Far from being passive commentators or spectators many of us were part of the events. Simultaneously we looked forward to insurgent strikes of a continental variety. And to a certain degree it's been blazing away for months.

So as the strike enters the winter months with the possibility of power cuts, we put forward these as yet rough suggestions to genuine revolutionaries and anarchists who aren't of the wally variety!

● To organise from within the movement, as we've done in the past by word of mouth and the usual informal contacts meetings involving delegates from as many trustworthy anarchist groups as possible.

● Planning deliberate spectacular mini-riots as soon as the power cuts arrive. (Or, failing that, late afternoon darkness.) The aim being to spark off trouble in the major urban areas, thus drawing police out of the mining areas.

HOW TO ACHIEVE this worthy task

As proved on the July anti-Reagan demo we can cause thousands of pounds worth of damage without suffering a single arrest, if well planned and co-ordinated. Judging by 'Stop the City' turnouts and our own interventions we can raise a force of at least 200 in London alone. This may be a conservative estimate. Obviously we don't intend squandering people in a face-to-face confrontation, as we may need to repeat the performance. Besides, we're not of the martyr material. In case the sceptical reader may wonder how such a plan could be achieved, here's a brief scenario. Of course it's only by comrades working together that we can oil out the mechanics of the operation:

● Thanks to the Electricity Board publicising where blackouts occur, we could assemble in a certain area at a pre-arranged time. Any sign of abnormal police presence would mean postponement.

● The ideal area would be a shopping area such as a high street. The crowds providing perfect cover when assembling our teams. Plenty of escape routes would be necessary. Gloves, scarfs and balaclavas wouldn't arouse suspicious during the winter.

● At a prearranged signal upon the advent of lights-out, the mob could condense within seconds, swinging into action. Parked cars should be dragged across the road, turned over, or even set alight, forming barricades, and causing traffic chaos there by making police access more difficult. Windows must be smashed, looting encouraged. Those police first on the scene, if small in number, could be resisted with bricks and other throwable material. Before they can gather sufficient strength, again at a prearranged signal, we'd disperse into the darkness.

● Headlines captured, it wouldn't take long for the example to spread. Against this background we'd blend, time to add our political dimensoin.

● Propaganda urging the opening of a second front, with the attendant looting and rioting, must appear beforehand. It should be made clear that these actions are a deliberate effort to spread class conflict as opened by the miners' strike. While the spreading of propaganda is an important task, we can't afford to dilute our numbers by having some engaging in their own individual actions simultaneously as has happened in recent times. Not only do they draw numbers away but these alternative actions mysteriously fail to appear. As a side interest this would show who really meant business and who was all mouth. No one group should lead it, this is our common task. We've just contributed with this suggestion, now's the time to discuss the matter seriously.

There is no alternative as far as we can see. It's all right to sloganise about setting up factory committees or community councils and call for a general strike. As these don't seem to be materialising it all remains a comfortable abstraction. We're not the vanguard but as a tiny fraction of the class the plan mapped out above is the only realistic action we can indulge ourselves in, gain results for the miners AND ourselves.

WE HAVE OUR OWN IDEA

OF TIME AND MOTION

MacGregor is KO'd

THESE were the terrifying moments yesterday when Coal Board chief Ian MacGregor faced the fury of 600 angry miners.

He was knocked unconscious as police escorted him through demonstrators protesting at pit closures.

One demonstrator shouted: "We will hear what he has to say, then we will tear his head off".

WE SHOULD HAVE FINISHED THE FUCKING BASTARD OFF THERE AND THEN!

Have you ever noticed how in leftie
papers they only ever print pictures
of miners being beaten up by the police?
They never use pictures that would
really cheer us up of the police being
given a good kicking or being carted off
to hospital. They always portray us
as passive victims of police violence.
Then they come up with a load of moral
crap about how nasty the cops are ...
as if we should be surprised about it!
Just occasionally they will say that
people fought back against the coppers
but this is only when they've been
attacked first by the police and had to
use self-defence! They continually seek
to justify morally any violence used
against the police.

LOOK WANKERS...we don't need
any moral justification to
attack the cops, we won't wait
to be attacked before we fight
back. The police and the bosses
are the enemies of the working
class and class violence is not
a moral issue but a necessary
part of our daily struggle to
get rid of these bastards.
Class violence never needs to
be justified...it just needs to be
carried out more often! We
need to attack first, not be on
the defensive. The lefties can sob
themselves to sleep about
pictures of beaten up miners
or memories of Blair Peach. We'll
never print this crap in Class
War. But pictures of
smashed up coppers or bosses...
yes please...we look forward to
the time when we can fill
the whole paper with them!!

54 Decade of DISORDER

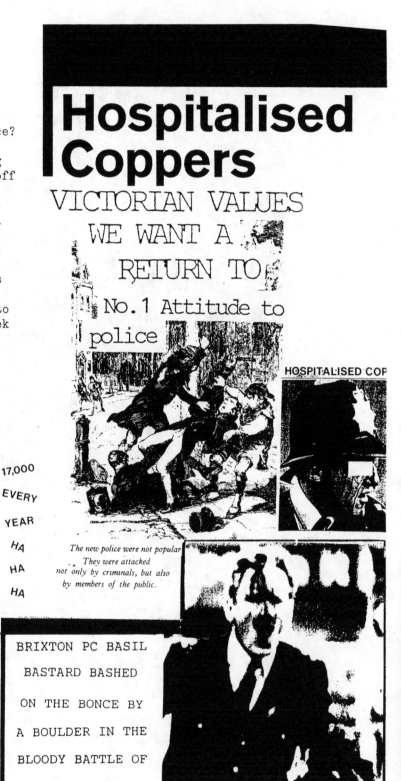

Hospitalised Coppers

VICTORIAN VALUES
WE WANT A
RETURN TO
No.1 Attitude to
police

17,000
EVERY
YEAR
HA
HA
HA

HOSPITALISED COP

*The new police were not popular
They were attacked
not only by criminals, but also
by members of the public.*

BRIXTON PC BASIL
BASTARD BASHED
ON THE BONCE BY
A BOULDER IN THE
BLOODY BATTLE OF
THE BARRIER BLOCK

HOSPITALISED COPPER
BACK BY POPULAR DEMAND

ANOTHER COPPER COPS IT!

HOSPITALISED COPPER

PC ARTHUR ARSEHOLE, AFTER BEING ATTACKED WITH A ARF BRICK AT THE ANTI-ARPARTHEID DEMO......HE CAN COME AND ACHE IN OUR AMBULANCE ANYTIME!!

AAAARGH!!

This issue's lovely page three fella, is none other than gorgeous, pouting, Sir Peter Imbert, Chief Commissioner of the Met!

Poor old Pete had a heart attack whilst out horse riding in Hyde Park!

The news that he's in intensive care fills us all full of sorrow. And we heartily deplore those members of the working class who have been;

● Phoning his house and asking for the "widow Imbert".

● Sending coffins and wreaths to his home.

● And we strongly recommend against phoning the hospital, pretending to be his wife, and saying you want the life support machine switched off!

HOSPITALISED

BATTERED
BOBBY
BILLY
BRUISED
AND BEATEN
IN BRISTOL
BUNDLE.

COPPER No12

OH HI, I'M YOUR SOCIAL WORKER.

LOOK, I'D TERRIFICALLY LIKE TO HELP YOU IN ANYWAY

GREAT, TAKE THIS BOTTLE AND WHEN THE COPPER COMES ROUND THE CORNER HIT 'IM WITH IT.

Demolish The

The biggest prison riots in British history! with Strangeways leading the way the working class in Britain's jails said "Enough is enough we ain't going to take this shit any longer" and promptly started on the only prison reform programme that we support – demolition!

What happened in the prisons was not just a riot – it was an uprising. As the liberals and the Left whinge on about the answer being nicer prisons we know different. Working class people inside, and outside prisons have had enough of unemployment, boredom, frustration, poverty, poll tax etc, etc.

Prison is much like life on the outside, the system can only work if we agree to let it, in other words if we consent to it. But things are changing, the politicians and the bosses have cranked up the odds in the class war that they are fighting against us to such an extent that many in our class are now faced with a clear cut choice: fight back or go under. To their great honour the prisoners decided to fightback. Many had a great deal to lose, especially those on remand.

PRISON and the WORKING CLASS

The vast majority of people in nick are working class people, there because they broke the laws designed to keep us all in our place. Meanwhile the real criminals, the bosses, are free to steal our work, kill us in wars, cause poverty and misery, loot the Third World etc, etc.

One of the most important things about the prison uprising was the growth in support on the outside. At

P isons

Strangeways hundreds gathered to show solidarity and give support to help to keep the men going. This is excellent, because the media try to persuade us that we have nothing in common with the people inside. They say they are animals who should be shot down, that the army should go in.

The fact is most people inside nicks are not a threat to our class. Many are in for petty crimes like nicking cars or non-payment of fines. We don't take the view that everyone inside is a wonderful person, that's romantic crap. But we do take the view that people are in prison because of their class.

LAW & ORDER or JUSTICE?

People go to prison because they break the law – simple. But those laws are there to protect the rich and their property. If you steal from the rich or the state you'll go down for a long time (like the train robbers), if you hurt or kill a rich person you'll go down for a long time (possibly life).

When it comes to us, the courts don't care if we rob or kill each other, but they have to go through the motions of justice to keep us believing in it. When it comes to crimes working class people are really worried about, violence against the old, women and children, the courts always give shorter sentences than crimes against property. Remember Judge Pickles who said a woman who was raped was "asking for it" or the Marine who recently shot his wife and baby dead, and walked from the court after a ticking off.

JUSTICE

If we want justice we have to do it ourselves. We don't mean revenge or gangs of 'vigilantes', which is what we have now. Instead of their sick morality, we have our own values. In a nutshell they can be called SOLIDARITY. We have to argue for this in our class and act accordingly.

This means you don't steal from your own, you don't beat or bully people who are weak, you don't put people down for being black, you don't treat women as inferior and you don't put people down for being gay.

Those in our class who break the solidarity of our class should know they will suffer for it.

CHASING THE COPS OUT...

...AND KEEPING THEM OUT!

What do we do when the cops FUCK OFF?

For most of us, the most important political events of the past five years have occurred, not in the smoke-filled rooms of the union barons; not in the stripped-pine rooms of the Habitat socialists; not even in the meat-free living spaces of the anarchist ghettoes, but on the streets and estates of the urban working class. From the blazing summer of 1981, through the miners strike, to the siege of Broadwater Farm, literally thousands of working class people have taken on the forces of darkness and the state, physically resisting the filth in a host of struggles, many of them suppressed by snivelling hacks. And we've only seen the preliminary skirmishes in a conflict as inevitable as it will be bloody.

URBAN WAR

Whether Kinnock, Thatcher or Owen scratch their way to the top of the parliamentary dungheap matters bugger all. By 1999, the urban war will be a permanent feature of everyday life in every benighted city on this septic isle.

There will be guns and deaths on both sides, as the cops mutate into daleks, and a host of scrapheap geniuses become the weaponsmiths of the ghettoes. The army will be there, either in an advisory/intelligence role (as they were in Brixton in 1981), or on the streets dressed as cops (as they were in the miners strike), or both. Increasingly, the cost of maintaining civil order, both in casualties and finance, will be more than the state is prepared to pay in the rotting heartlands of our cities.

FANTASY AND REALITY

This all sounds fine as apocalyptic fantasy, but what's it going to be like when YOU have no choice about living it . . . 24 hours a day? It's already too close for comfort for some of us. While the police terrorise Broadwater Farm, stealing food and clothing, and menacing people with guns, people living on the Gloucester Grove estate in Peckham, South London, are deprived of post and emergency services due to attacks by anti-social elements. If we're not careful, the 1990s in the cities

could be a choice between these two options – occupation by brutal psycho-cops or terrorisation by criminal scum.

The two rapes in the 1985 Brixton riot underline this point. Writing in the magazine Monochrome, a woman refers to women being treated as "the spoils of war" and describes how she felt safer fighting the cops than being in the area they'd been kicked out of. Well, sod that for a liberated zone!

WHAT DO WE DO WHEN THE COPS FUCK OFF?

The question of what we're actually going to DO when the cops fuck off has been almost completely ignored by street revolutionaries, but it's one of the most important problems we face. There is no way that people are going to be grateful to see the back of the filth, if they think that muggers, rapists, smack-dealers, wife beaters, and other anti-social bastards are going to have a free hand.

But it needn't be like that. Someone once told me of an incident he witnessed in occupied Ireland. Rioting on the Falls road had carried on 'til early morning, and vehicles

were needed for a road-block, when along whirred a milk float. Quick as a flash it was commandeered. However, it was not torched until the crates had been taken off and every local household had been delivered two pints of milk!

COMMUNITY RESISTANCE

This sort of interaction between street-fighters and the rest of the community is essential. When looting takes place, we must make sure that goods are distributed to those in need, not as an abstract matter of principle, but because we need to show that we care far more about the welfare of our fellow prisoners in the slum streets and rat-hole estates than any number of incompetent, grassing social workers. And, of course, in a state of insurrection, those who look after our kids, carry messages and weapons, lie for us in court, and give first-aid are as vital to the struggle as the able-bodied, young, and largely

estates will continue to fall for all that law 'n' order bullshit.

IT STARTS NOW!

It starts now. With thinking about what you'd do if you saw next door being broken into. There's got to be a better answer than calling the cops or letting it happen. And we need to find it before every street has a neighbourhood watch snoop snivelling back to the smiling community bobby with his plastic bullets and computer files.

It starts now. With making sure that in this summer's riots, the muggers are challenged, and the rapists eliminated. With making sure that clumsiness or drunken stupidity don't result in proper people getting their homes burnt out.

It starts now. With discussions on the streets and estates about what we are going to do when the cops fuck off. Street justice is justice for ALL, by ALL. Anything else is just a new set of cops. We need the answers quickly, and we haven't begun to ask the right questions.

male (though less so every time!) streetfighters.

But it's not just a question of handing out a few tins of beans to the old folk. If we cannot deliver safe streets and secure homes for EVERYONE, ordinary people will be begging for the return of the law. Obviously informers must be dealt with severely, but the best way to stop them creeping out of the woodwork is to prove that the community can do a better job of preventing anti-social behaviour than the filth.

STREET JUSTICE

Street Justice is an ugly phrase. It carries visions of Clint Eastwood, crazed vigilantes shooting black kids for being assertive; the IRA kneecapping kids for smoking dope; the Ayatollah's "Party of God" beating women for daring to dress the way they want. But, somewhere along the line, as individuals, as communities and as a class, we are going to have to learn how to dispense street justice. Otherwise, people terrified to walk their own streets and

Salford Calling

In the last issue of Class War, we told you how some of the residents of Salford, Manchester, were getting together to drive anti-social elements out of their community.

They were banding together not only to get rid of the muggers, conmen who pray on old folk and people who burgle off other working class people, but also to get rid of the police, the filth who protect the rich (the real criminals) and keep us in our place, the bottom.

Earlier in the year there was a series of large demonstrations against the police in Salford. They were directed against police brutality and heavy handedness, often these demonstrations turned violent as the police tried, and failed, to clear the streets.

The result was a memorable "public meeting" between the police and youths. The top cop in Salford, Jim Tunmer, ended the meeting in uproar after telling the youths "if you want war, you've got war!"

All this was too much for the Greater Manchester Police, they "retired" Tunmer, and moved out most of the riot units from the Ordsall estate. Since "Jolly Jim's" retirement Salford's finest have moved into the Precinct area.

There, once again, they met with the violent opposition from the residents and youths of this designers' nightmare. With, at the very least, 35 blocks of flats occupied mainly by the young unemployed and low waged.

The terror tactics of the law weren't appreciated. Salford's Robo Cops cruised up and down the Broadwalk public pathway, harassing people in their way, and giving everyone a hard time. The fact they used riot T.A.G. units for this made matters worse.

People were getting more and more pissed off with them. Eventually, the flashpoint came when a car chase through the estate saw at least ten cops cars screaming through the streets. People began attacking the police with anything they could lay their hands on, it was the start of a week's rioting.

As the days passed police were met with petrol bombs and burning barricades. They responded by running amok, their ID numbers covered, lashing out at anybody with their batons.

In the photo, right, are some kids from the Ordsall estate in Salford. They're about to throw a stuffed Yuppie (unfortunately not a real one) on to a bonfire. A couple

such Yuppies were thrown onto bonfires on November 5th. never mind Guy Fawkes, as you can see by the smiles on their faces - this was a lot more fun!

Breakaway groups of youths peeled off to attack the police station, they were successful! Eventually, the battle lost, the T.A.G. units were withdrawn, off to another estate. Where hopefully they'll meet the same resistance.

In an interview with Class War, one local youth summed up the mood; "The youths round here have realised that the majority of duties carried out by the police are either a trivial, timewasting load of bollocks, designed to keep us down, or are spent protecting the rich bastards in Salford Quays.

"The youth of Salford have been making one thing clear since the start of the year. *We are capable of sorting out our own problems within the community, by the community.*

"Burglars, rapists, muggers, con-artists and all the other socially unacceptable scum who pray on the old, the weak or the other working class residents will NO LONGER BE TOLERATED! The beating of burglars has already started, and some people have put up a £500 reward so that we can catch, and drive out these people. There is no place within Salford for them.

OUR CONTRIBUTION
TO GLOBAL WARMING

After
The Riot

The recent riots in Brixton, Tottenham, Handsworth and St. Pauls were all basically for the same reason – to re-establish *our* control over *our* territory and drive the cops out.

In this the riots have been successful, but the aftermath of the uprisings have been far from 'utopian'.

The Tories and other right-wingers have started calling for *more* policing, heavier sentences and repatriation – none of which help the local working class.

The Labour Party and the lefties start spouting their patronising racism, hijacking the situation and setting up pathetic 'Police Monitoring Groups'. The police, of course, continue to go their own sweet way doing exactly what they want, i.e. keeping the working class in their place whilst claiming to protect and serve them.

Meanwhile the riot zone ends up as a lawless, crime-ridden area, with locals getting mugged and their homes robbed, and local crime barons seizing control and establishing *their* dictatorship of the area, through fear and intimidation.

None of this is of any benefit to the people and their community. It plays right into the hands of the police and authorities because – despite their justified mistrust of the police – the people end up wanting the cops back.

This gives the police the perfect opportunity to invade the area like an occupying army, re-establishing their control over the local working class.

A choice between the cops, Tory and Labour policies and crime-barons is no choice at all!

We must take the initiative and responsibility of policing our communities ourselves.

If people are to struggle to defend their own community then they've got to think it is worth fighting for. In many inner city areas it is quite natural that people do not believe their communities are worth defending, ridden as they are with mugging, burglary, smack dealing and general isolation and fear.

We have to offer practical solutions to such problems as crime on estates . . . solutions which are not pious hopes but which can offer the prospect of immediate relief of the problem. The obvious answer is for the people to police their own estates and deal with the anti-social elements themselves. This raises the issue of who controls the estate . . . the tenants or the police? The vital task is for the tenants to take control away from the police and council and run their estates themselves in conjunction with local authority workers.

We must create situations of dual power where the councils may retain nominal power but in reality it is the tenants who are in control. Then such areas can become no-go areas for police, council officials, Government bureaucrats, bailiffs, rent collectors but also for muggers, rapists and other anti-social elements that shit on their own kind. Once a sense of community feeling is established in an area then people will quite naturally proceed to resist advancing Yuppies and attempts to drive them out. Their sense of themselves as a class with culture worth fighting for will give them the confidence to act in a combative manner and go from defence to offence.

The question of who controls not just an estate but entire working class areas will become increasingly contested. From this a strenghtened class consciousness and combativity will emerge which begins to challenge control of society as a whole.

This Was CLASS WAR

Anyone RICH was Attacked

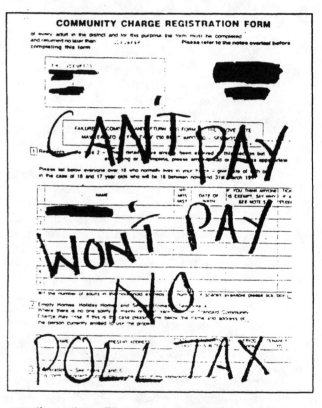

WHAT A DAY!...FUCKIN BRILLIANT...
THE BEST SATURDAY OUT EVER!?
Saturday 31st March 1990, the day
before the hated Tory tax came into being in England and Wales,and a massive
anti poll tax march in central London became a mass
uprising of class anger!

There's very little more to be said about the London
uprising. If you were there, you'll never forget the day
that we took central London, gave the cops a right batter-
ing, and then took the class war to the plush shops and
cars of the idle rich, right in the heart of the city!

Right from the start the cops were totally unprepared
for the onslaught of class anger that was coming their
way. They pissed about in the sun thinking that the
250,000 people on the march were just going to listen to
a few whingeing speakers, and then get on their coaches
and go home. How wrong could they be!

For years we've been told to shut up, stay put, and do
as we're told, as our class suffers under the barrage of
Tory policy. The miners were left out in the cold by the
Labour Party, as were the printers, seamen and

countless others. They turned the full force of the state
upon us, and expected us to passively do as were told.

Well not any more, now is when we go on the offensive!
Even the authorities admitted that there were over 3,000
people in the forefront of the rioting! The sheer scale of
the police injuries (over 350) testifies to that, as does the
damage done (millions of pounds worth).

For days later TV screens were full of pictures of burnt
out yuppie cars, smashed posh shops, and tearful faces
of the idle rich as they came to terms with the mass out-

THIS IS THE REAL
COMMUNITY
CHARGE!

BUY THIS
WOMAN
A DRINK !!

break of class anger, on the very streets that they count as their own!

Make no mistake, this was no drunken mob, or the high spirited actions of a few kids, this was MASS CLASS WAR.

As the filth forced Trafalgar Square clear, the mobs went in different directions. East to the plush arcades of Covent Garden. North to the expensive shopping areas of Regent St. West to Leicester Square. All with the same motive, to show the rich scum exactly what we think of them, and what they can expect more of in the future!

The battles on the streets with the riot cops weren't the actions of a few scared kids. They were the actions of a working class tired of being trampled on by both the money-grabbing Capitalists of the Right, and the back-stabbing, hypocrites of the Left. They were the actions of people proud to say they've done their bit for the class war, proud to battle with the forces of the state as they try to suffocate us under yet another class aimed law.

This was no "drunken mob riot", this was class war . . . and they'd better get used to it.

Make Them Pay

BAILIFFS...

MAKE MY DAY!
NO POLL TAX HERE

The Poll Tax is the most ambitious attack the Tories have made on the working class since they came to power.

In order to defeat it the response has to be just as ambitious. Class War has argued over and over again for the tactics currently being used in many areas of the country, and is pleased to see them working to a large extent. So what are these tactics, and how will they beat the poll tax, and why do we want to defeat the thing in the first place?

The trouble outside town halls in the last few weeks led to EVERY political party, including Militant, falling over themselves in the rush to condemn the violence. Even the Federation of Anti Poll Tax Unions moaned about how awful it all was. The violence is started by locals, angry at the council setting a rate. Let's face it, the SWP or Militant can't be behind it, they haven't got the guts. They seriously believe peaceful protest is enough, IT IS NOT! The rioting in Hackney set the pound plunging on the international money markets, this is how much power the working class have!

Scraps with cops outside town halls may not stop the Poll Tax, but they're good confidence builders and who needs an excuse for a fight with the bill? Resisting collecting of the Poll Tax *will* stop its implementation. The only way to resist the onslaught of poll tax offices, bailiffs, police and the courts is by collective community action. We must organise to stop them collecting off any of us. "Reception committees" for bailiffs, asking the postie to lose summonses, occupations of local housing offices. We have to make every attempt to collect one person's poll tax cost them thousands of pounds in bailiffs' wages, admin costs, police manpower, they'll soon give in.

So how do we fight back against these 20th Century robber barons? In Scotland they have developed networks of people to run and ring round peoples' houses at the first sign of the bailiffs. Huge groups of people have been assembled in this way, and the council thugs frightened off.

BUY THIS MAN A DRINK !

The time to start calling on your neighbours though is not when the first furniture auction happens down your street, it is NOW! People should be going round, knocking on doors to see who is willing to help and in what way, assembling the technology needed to fight a modern day community battle, mobile phones, CB radios (remember them), typewriters (to combat lies in the local press) etc . . .

These things don't cost money, if you look hard enough you'll find people with access to all sorts of things. The battle against the Poll Tax will be fought and won on the streets, lobbies of parliament and petitions are a waste of time!

The fight against the Poll Tax will defeat the attempt to make the rich prosper at the expense of the working class, it could also lead to the creation of stronger, safer, more friendly communities. This is the real threat to the ruling class, because a strong working class is a threat to their power.

For us victory against the poll tax could be the opportunity to start changing some of the other shit we've put up with under this lunatic economic system.

POLL TAX
FLAGSHIP SUNK

GOTCHA!

Their Politics

SPOT THE DIFFERENCE

GRANDPA MUNSTER   NORMAN LAMONT

TRICK QUESTION - THERE ISN'T ONE - THEY'RE BOTH BLOODSUCKERS!

What's all this bollocks about John Major being "classless", as TV presenters and everyone else are fond of calling him?

With the Labour Party spending the last 5 or 6 years chasing the Guardian-reading Green voters, it must be easy for the cosseted media pundits to think that Major is so-called "classless".

But would you think of your Bank Manager or some top civil servant as "classless", of course not!

PRIVILEGED

Just because he doesn't have a long-winded title, or isn't heir to some country estate, doesn't mean that he's working class, or "classless" in Tory-speak.

In the eighties the Tories tried to tell us all that we were all middle class, now in the nineties we are supposed to be seeing the "classless society".

What a load of crap! John Major has had the privileged life of someone who came from a well-off middle class family, and was educated in a top Surrey Grammar School.

He knew which side of the bread was buttered, and has spent his entire life climbing up the Establishment ladder – local Tory Councillor, senior bank manager, kids in posh public school etc. etc. – what's so surprising that he became Prime Minister?

MYTH

Like Thatcher before him, he will serve his Establishment bosses well until, like her, his usefulness ends, then out will come the Mark II model. And off we'll go on the merry-go-round of so-called Parliamentary Democracy all over again.

The most vital part of maintaining this myth of democracy is that change is seen to happen, whilst the reality is that REAL change NEVER happens.

Part of this must be a change of leadership every now and then – Thatcher/Major, Tory/Labour – it doesn't matter who's captain of the ship, because the hands on the steering wheel are still the same.

SPOT THE LACK OF DIFFERENCES

ALRIGHT WE ACCEPT THERE ARE DIFFERENCES. THE ONE ON THE RIGHT WOULD MAKE A BETTER PRIME MINISTER!

NEIL KINNOCK   **SLIME MONSTER**

Rancid Ruling Class

ONE OF THE MOST SICKENING THINGS ABOUT THATCHER'S RESIGNATION WAS THE WAY MPS OF EVERY PARTY REVELLED IN PRAISING HER.

The House of Commons was full of 637 fawning lickspittles, all rushing to pay honour to her "statesmanship and good sense".

We have suffered 11 years of the parasite, now she's being treated like a modern-day Churchill, by the party that will probably be next to govern, Labour.

BOOED!

One of the most encouraging things was the crowds that gathered outside Downing St, once the news was released, and booed and jeered Thatcher as she left to go to the Palace to tell the Queen.

But at the end of the day, Thatcher or no Thatcher, Hurd, Major or Heseltine, it *makes sod all different to our lives.*

Marg or butter, Labour or Tory, Gazza or Ninja Turtles, Kuwait or Iraq – an endless parade of false choices. In this way the essential illusion of freedom of choice within capitalism is maintained: the bedrock on which the entire system rests.

CLASS WAR SAYS: BOLLOCKS TO THIS!

As long as all we can do is slavishly respond to the agenda which the ruling class sets for us, we are doomed to impotence.

At the next general election the left will say "vote Labour". *WE SAY:*

CRAP!

We won't choose from any of the festering dungheaps on offer. Thazzeltine or Paddy Kinnochio. They're all destined for the same shit chute!

As the 70s refrain went: *"Edward Wilson, Harold Heath, them on top, us underneath".*

We have to set our own agenda, now.

Our "election campaign" has already begun. It's out on the streets, in our communities, every time the poll tax bailiffs appear; it's on the streets of London March 30th 1990, for the biggest, most combative demonstration ever; it's outside every Town Hall in the country on General Election night to make *THEM* shudder with *OUR POWER. CLASS WAR SAYS THIS, AND ONLY THIS:*

ENOUGH IS ENOUGH!

We're gonna shift the rancid ruling class from off our backs for once and for all.

Let those bastards shake and quiver with fear in their mansions and penthouses...*OUR TIME IS FAST APPROACHING!*

Militant Grasses to THE FILTH

The papers have been full of how the Anti Poll Tax Campaign is being run by a load of left wing nutty extremists. The best known of these is the "Militant Tendency" with their paper "Militant" (original eh!).

Militant have been around for 20 years and basically believe that they should inflitrate the Labour Party with enough "good socialists" (their supporters) to vote "socialism" into existence. They are into a theory of "Transitional Demands" which means demanding the impossible or things unlikely to happen, like Kinnock should support non-payment of the poll tax, which makes Militant look like good socialists. When the Labour Party start trying to expel them, like when they bankrupted Liverpool council and started laying off council workers, we are all meant to rally to their support – but no one did! Tough Luck Suckers!

In a desperate attempt to relaunch itself back into the forefront of the Labour Party the machinery of Militant has geared up to building a campaign around the Poll Tax, but more importantly *around itself*.

A few weeks ago local councils met to set the poll tax. Militant were begging Labour councils not to prosecute non payers even though these same councils have already recruited teams of bailiffs! This is typical of Militant, their strategies are crap and consist of making futile demands which only divert attention and energy away from the real struggle on the street. Anybody who thinks that the Labour Party can be forced to act in our interests needs their head examining. The means of resistance to this tax, the bailiffs and the cops, exists in our communities NOT in the Left and their parties. Mili-

tant's goal is a "Socialist Labour Party", even if they could achieve it, we don't need or want one thanks very much. But rest assured that when they've no more use for the Anti-Poll Tax campaign Militant will disregard it and start looking for the "next big thing".

The other left wing party involved in the anti-poll tax campaign is the, wait for it, SOCIALIST WORKERS' PARTY. The extent of their involvement is limited to giving out placards, chanting boring slogans and trying to sell their bog-roll quality paper whilst local working class people are smashing down town hall doors. The SWP's idea of action is to chant "Maggie, Maggie, Maggie – Out, Out, Out" whilst everyone else is getting stuck in (apart from Militant, who run away when the batteries on their megaphones go).

They both offer us nothing, they and the rest of the "extreme left" say the same thing – do nothing and wait.

We don't want to kick the
Tories out...we just want
to kick them!!

BIRDS PUT THE TURD IN CUSTARD

BUT WHO PUT THE SHIT IN NO. 10?

KINNOCHIO SPEAKS

DO NOTHING...
BLAH...BLAH...
DON'T FIGHT BACK
BLAH...BLAH...
LET THE POLICE
BEAT YOU UP

The left have learnt and can
learn nothing. They propose
another five years of chanting
and marching, starting on election
night when a small group of
fucking idiots greeted Thatcher
back to Downing St with cries of
'Maggie,Maggie,Maggie...Out,Out,
Out...'(TWATS).
     We don't want to kick the Tories
out...we just want to kick them!!
The middle class lefties can

continue their politics as hobby,
single issue,peace camp CND,
Greens/Ecologyllifestyle,Embrace
a base every bank holiday,City
Limits every Thursday,Guardian
every day.
     When the cruise missiles go in
they'll still be prancing,dancing
and singing their way round in
circles. There can no longer be
any turning back to the remedies
of the left for us.

FIve MORe YEARS
of thiS SHiT..?

unemployed stayed in bed on polling day

NO FUcKing WAY!

WANKERS

Toxteth residents in a
hurry to support their
local labour council?...
You've gotta be joking !

The Left: Part of the Problem

NOT THE SOLUTION

Class War has never gone for the Left's shopping list of 101 good causes. We never supported the 'progressive' or 'socialist' dictatorships of Castro or Mugabe, China or Vietnam any more than we did Walesa or Gorbachev, Ortega or Mandela. We didn't toast the ANC in Nicaraguan coffee for we knew that the Comrades of Soweto would soon have to wage their struggle against Mandela managed capitalism as fiercely as they fought against de Klerk. We didn't support Saddam Hussein in the bosses war for oil in the Gulf any more than we did Bush or Major. Certainly we advocated 'Shoot the Enemy' – but they were the officers on both sides!

Unlike the Left we do not support what we don't want, with or without 'illusions'. For us our enemy's enemy is not automatically our friend. We only support what we want worldwide – autonomous working class struggle wherever and whenever it rears its lovely head. Otherwise we do not choose between our oppressors.

At home it is a mark of Thatcher's success that she has pulled the whole of the opposition along on her ideological coatails. The Labour party of Kinnock and Gould is a yuppie party populated by designer socialists – Kinnock is a right wing bastard who could well end up a more useful tool for the bosses than a wet Tory party.

In London boroughs such as Hackney and Islington the Labour Councils have savaged services to the working class, left thousands of homes empty, evicted squatters and adopted hare-brained schemes for institutionalised anti-racism and anti-sexism which are loathed by the working class

In the wake of the yuppified Labour Party the rest of the Left has trailed behind. *Marxism Today*, with its wine lists, articles about how 'the working class no longer exists' – except to scrub their fucking Habitat stripped pine floors, and skiing holidays, has cornered the market in trendy intellectuals who want to play at being revolutionaries but still enjoy all the benefits of a privileged position within consumer capitalism. The Socialist Workers Party is now populated by teachers, probation officers and university lecturers.

Marx

Spencer

Mickey Mouse

Leon Trotsky

Lenin

McCartney

MARX LENNON

57 varieties

All unfit for
human consumption

The oppositional malaise of the Left flows from this fact – that their class composition makes them incapable of a sustained fightback since if it did it would be against their own class interest. Thus when it comes to the crunch they will all advocate voting Labour despite the fact that they have been slagging off the very same Labour party for the last four years. No wonder the working class has no faith in their ideas which usually extend no further than the preservation of their own interests dressed up as a political campaign e.g. save their well paid job with the local council. The fact that the working class will not strike to defend the jobs of their local anti-racism council officer remains a complete mystery to them.

To make 'demands' on any of these people to do this or that on behalf of the working class makes no more sense than demanding that the TUC calls a general strike or that the trade unions act in the interests of their members. They are part of the problem not the solution.

CND = Wankers

BombsNotJobs

IF YOU THINK BUILDING CHAPELS,
PLANTING SEEDS, AND PUTTING
BALLOONS ON FENCES CAN STOP
NUCLEAR WEAPONS... THEN YOU'RE
A FUCKING IDIOT.

IF YOU WANT PEACE PREPARE FOR WAR

NICE IMAGE, NICE SMILES
NICE SCARVES, NICE HAIRSTYLES
NICE POLITICS . . . .
NICE FUCKIN' TRY ARSE'OLES !!

Y looked like sisters yesterday, as Labour
r Neil Kinnock's wife Glenys and CND
man Joan Ruddock displayed the same
swept hairstyle, the same smiles and the
scarves.

ROCK Against THE RICH

```
"I'm doing this tour for myself. I can't pick
up the guitar if I'm on an ego trip ... I didnt
pick up no guitar to be some commercial bastard.
I believe in  Rock 'n Roll...I believe it
speaks beyond commercial limits...I believe a
limit should be put on the property developers.
They're driving people out of the city centres.
Someones gotta fight for people who can't
afford their ridiculous prices... it's insane!
There's gotta be a stop to it.
   It's a good chaotic idea.I'm not a person who
has any sense   of responsibility. I'm compre-
hensibly irresponsible as I suspect most
musicians are. So I liked the idea from the
word go.
              Joe Strummer.
```

At a time when rock music and its surrounding cults and causes are about as threatening as a bowl of marshmallows, Class War has initiated *Rock against the rich* in a concerted attempt to put class politics back onto the political agenda, using music as a weapon.

Of course, the idea of using music to bring people together under one roof and pass on ideas is not a new one. However, protest in musical terms now means little more than a tally-ho collection of former tax-exiles regurgitating a load of "isn't it awful" rhetoric about injustices in some far off land. And, with the exception perhaps of "Live Aid", the majority of working class people have shown little interest.

Unfortunately the overall political situation is even less inspiring. While the Tory government is calling all the shots, the "opposition" is showing itself to be permanently on the defensive.

With a Labour Party that put the "dead" into deadwood, containing more yuppies than a Sloane Square knees-up, and the rest of 'the left' revealing themselves to be about as relevant as a jar of caviar at a miners'

gala, the prospects of a credible opposition to Thatcherism seem paper thin.

However, something utterly ruthless has arisen from this despair. Something that goes far beyond the realms of parliamentary politics . . . Yes! it's *Rock against the rich!*

We want to take politics back to the grassroots, the nitty-gritty. To the people who are really "facing the music" in terms of their daily struggles.

We are organising benefits for communities and people involved in the *real* fightback – not some poxy leftie excuse for one.

The time to seize back control of our lives, communities and workplaces, and then ruthlessly hunt down our class enemies is now.

Let's rock against the rich! e.g. In North Wales RAR will be supporting villagers resisting the takeover of their areas by holiday homes for the rich; in South Wales RAR will support local communities involved in robbing coal trains – repossessing what their own class dug from the ground in the first place; in Doncaster there will be a benefit for sacked miners, and in Dover for sacked P&O

ROCK AGAINST THE RICH
TOUR 88

JOE STRUMMER
TO HEADLINE
NATIONAL R.A.R.
TOUR

workers and their families; in towns like Liverpool, Birmingham, Hull, Southampton, Newcastle and East London, where inner city and dockside areas are being yuppified, local people engaged in fightback against the Tories' Urban Development Corporations will be supported.

We believe that rock music can be a force in bringing people together for organised resistance. RAR is using music in a concrete way — the music is directly related to the political struggles of these working class communities where the concerts are staged. Wherever the working class are engaged in active resistance RAR will be doing gigs, inviting people in the struggles to speak.

RAMBLO !

Since the War, the pastime of rambling has had a middle class image.

Nowadays, it seems that you can't be a 'proper' walker unless you read all the right magazines and fork out lots of dosh for high-tech kit that looks like it was meant for walking on the moon!

But rambling has never been the exclusive pastime of the middle class. Working class people ENJOY going out for a stroll at the weekend and taking in a breath of fresh air.

Over recent years the increasing shittiness of the ruling class has resulted in landowners restricting and stopping access to open country.

Even the National Trust whine on about "too many walkers" eroding the land. What the fuck are they worried about! Afraid we might wear out the mountains and moors?

The irony is that while they deny us access to beautiful countryside on our doorsteps, the landowners are "developing" the countryside by creating more grouse-shooting moors or building more up-market housing for yuppies and the retired rich.

While people who were born in the country are being forced to move away to cities, because they can't afford the prices in their OWN towns, the countryside is becoming out of bounds to us except for the odd coach trip to a stately home or theme park. They might as well put fences around the cities to keep us in!

We must remember that we obtained the limited rights of access to the land we have because working class people challenged the power of the landlords in the 1930s by MASS TRESSPASS and hand-to-hand FIGHTING against hired thugs.

The most famous incident was the 'invasion' of Kinder Scout in the Peak District by 800 workers from Sheffield and Manchester when the landlord's heavies GOT A BEATING.

As the song says: "This land is our land, from shore to shining shore." WE intend to use it for OUR benefit.

The sight of the odd landlord hanging in the breeze has usually sorted out the problem in the past.

Dear William

   You have chosen to pollute East Coker by your occasional presence
at your holiday home. Not content with your unwanted gentrification
of the village, however, you have claimed to 'own' Pen Wood, and
deny access to local people, all people other than your lackeys,
in fact.
   Such anti-social behaviour can no longer be tolerated: On June
22, Pen Wood will be re-opened to public access by a mass trespass.
   We suggest that you could be well-advised not to attempt to tamper
with such access after this date.
   The anger of working class people in the rural areas against your
sort is growing. You might like to consider removing your presence
from East Coker altogether, while you still have time to effect an
orderly retreat.

Yours,

Captain Swing,
The Cave,
Pen Wood.

OPEN LETTER TO THE 'OWNER' OF PEN WOOD

Fuckwit

Hold the front page! Sir Randulph Twistleton-Feinnes is making yet another heroic expedition to conquer the North Pole! No, stop press! He's given up because – wait for it – IT'S TOO COLD!!

Well, what a fuckin shock that must of been. Last year Fuckwit gave up another attempt because – wait again – there was too much snow about!! What a stunner that was to us all, snow at the North Pole, the one eventuality he couldn't have bargained for.

Upper class, chinless wonder Fuckwit tries to portray himself as a brave individual pitting himself against the elements – forgetting to mention the small backup crew of rescue helicopters, support ships, TV crews, and a cast of a thousand paid lickspittles, financed by his polo playing chums!

Just like Richard Branson's ballooning, or pot-bellied Peter De Savary's Americas cup challenge. These millionaire adventurers like to pass off their rich man's hobbies as a sport we should all get excited about. We are supposed to clap and cheer these rich twats on their way. The only way we'd cheer is if a polar bear ate the bastard!!!

Watch our next issue for details of Class War's adventure to the South Pole to establish the democracy of the workers' councils amongst the penguins! All able bodied men and women to enlist. No time wasters. Oh yeah, it might be a bit cold and snowy!!!

Live Aid

We live in a world of surplus, yet everywhere millions are starving. Two-thirds of the world's population are malnourished, while in the West over-eating is one of our biggest killers, and still we have massive stockpiles of food which stay stuck in their warehouses because it is more profitable to the owners to hang on to it than to distribute it to those who need it. This sick joke is the reality of capitalism: that their filthy profits are more important than people. The history of an elite, our so-called social betters, come before the interests of the poor who live under them, those like us at the bottom of the pile. The capitalist machine is fuelled by overconsumption and greed, and just as they exploit and abuse their own workers, they systematically do it abroad, resulting in, for the people of the Third World, destruction of their old lifestyles and means of support. Because we cannot ignore this suffering that our system has created in Africa we must occasionally wash our consciences through public spectacles like Live Aid. Of course it is great that some money is raised to help feed people, yet really it is nothing but a smokescreen to hide the real problems and the faces of the guilty. Live Aid provides no future for the people it claims to help. It papers over a few cracks but ignores the roots of the problem, it is nothing more than flinging the Ethiopians a few crumbs of 'our charity'.

The real way to end their suffering is to destroy the causes of exploitation wherever we find them; to destroy the power of the new slave masters of the Third World, the capitalist multinationals . . . corporations like IBM, Thorn, Coca Cola, Nestles etc. These corporations create more wealth for themselves while ripping off the poor left, right and centre, with the full approval of their governments and the people who claim to care for the Third World. Ethiopia has no future in the efforts of a bunch of pathetic, posing, filthy-rich pop stars, who help prop up the system of world exploitation, while mouthing trendy slogans about 'Feed the World', driving round in limousines and sniffing cocaine.

The only solution is to free the world of this disgusting system that has us all in its grip, of profits before people. This is not a time for charity but a time for political action against our rich oppressors.

Bastard Branson

AMONGST ALL THE SUFFERING THE GULF WAR IS CREATING, THERE ARE ALWAYS THOSE WHO SEEK TO GET IN ON THE ACT. ONE SUCH IS VIRGIN TYCOON RICHARD BRANSON.

What makes Branson tick, apart from money that is, is him getting his ugly face on TV etc. So when Iraq boss Saddam Hussein offered to let foreign nationals go, by being flown out, Branson must have been wetting his pants at the thought of all that publicity for the company (and boss) which flies them.

LICKSPITTLES

Branson, whose previous "daring" exploits include belting across the Atlantic, in a high powered boat, shadowed by hundreds of fawning lickspittles in every manner of boat and plane (even a satellite!), failing to even take off in an "epic" ego-tripping balloon ride, and being "minister for litter" in the failed Thatcher "bin it" campaign.

He must of thought his day had come! A few quick phone calls to the media, and Branson could be spotted

CLASS WAR balloon makers apologise most sincerely to Mr R Branson for the premature destruction of his hot air balloon, before it got off the ground.

It was of course designed to break up at 30,000 feet, whilst travelling at 300 mph, in mid-Pacific.

Unfortunately the two day delay meant the glue, which was designed to come unstuck well into the flight did so on the ground.

We have improved our workmanship and can assure Mr Branson that our new design is guaranteed to deflate in mid-flight.

We also do a good line in parachutes which all rich bastards are urged to wear when poncing about in a fuckin balloon while we're slaving about down here!

down on Runway One, clutching air stewardesses and bottles of champagne, in front of one of his company jets.

Relatives of the hostages were sickened: "A sick publicity stunt", said one, "If he's so concerned, why doesn't he give some of his millions to help the families?" said another.

People like Branson get a kick out of being seen as "world figures": they are the scum who play with people's lives to further their own ambitions.

If Saddam Hussein wants western nationals to use as so-called "shields" around army bases, then I can think of a few scumbags who won't be missed by anyone . . .

Whose Game Is It Anyway ?

MILLWALL DIAMONDS

"**T**HE NUTTERS OF THE LEAGUE"; "SCUM"; "EVIL". Just a few of the "compliments" paid to Millwall fans by the press following the violence at the FA Cup clash with Arsenal.

All we got in the papers were moans about how the chance of a return to Europe for English clubs had been wrecked by Millwall's "thugs".

However, compared to the '70s and the days when the "F-Troop" and "Treatment" hooligan gangs were attacking everything that moved (and most things that didn't) the trouble on January 9th was more of a minor tiff than the civil war portrayed in the press.

For years the Old Bill have been getting up Millwall fans' noses, and at Highbury it was decided to "blow a few of 'em out!"

For Lions fans, away games this season have been a nightmare of mile-long queues, mounted police trying to mow people down and endless body searches, only to be packed out sardine-style once you get in like at Upton Park and Highbury.

THE WRITINGS ON THE WALL.....
the full message at Fulham reads
"asset strippers are bastards".

Vinny 'nutsgrabber'
Jones when asked
by NME about the
best thing he ever
did during his days
as a hod carrier
replied; 'Dropping a LUMP HAMMER off
a roof onto a MERCEDES'.
Welcome to CLASS WAR Vinny!

Unfortunately, home games aren't much better. If it ain't enough to pay £3.50 to get into Coldblow Lane's answer to Colditz, then you've got the cops videoing every ones' mug for their secret "DIRTY DEN" operation. Then when a goal is scored and you jump for joy you get collared by the cops and dragged up to the "ejectory room" to be videoed, your particulars taken, and before being turfed out told that if you get hauled up again you'll be charged and banned for life.

How long before farting on the terraces constitutes a "Breach of the Peace"?!

However, this treatment is not reserved for Millwall fans. The same is taking place all around the country.

It is all part of an organised plot by the powers-that-be to snuff the life out of football fans and make them into a characterless mob of zombies whose only response to on-field activity can be "Oh-good!" or "Gosh!"

Football is for many working class people the only thing that unites them anymore, the only thing that still brings people together. It is this that scares the goverment; when working class people are united they are capable of anything, and this is why the authorities are acting as they are.

However, football supporters are not taking it lying down.

Scarves are going on faces to beat the video invasion. The press were on the receiving end of a bit of class justice the week after the Highbury incident for the lies they wrote. And the cops are increasingly coming under attack on the terraces with a firm "This is our territory — you aren't wanted here!"

It's up to us to make sure that football remains an enjoyable working class pastime, and doesn't get ruined by nutters, the cops or the leeches who pass for board members.

We are the real diamonds. The cops and directors are just a load of worthless cobble-stones who'll get walked over if they stick their noses in our affairs any further.

LET THE *REAL* SUPPORTERS RUN THE CLUBS!!

ASSes

THE ONLY PEOPLE WHO'LL
BENEFIT FROM ALL SEATERS

THE LATEST PET SCHEME OF THE EDITORIAL AND SPORTS WRITERS AND COLIN 'MR SUBBUTEO' MOYNIHAN IS ALL-SEATER FOOTBALL STADIUMS.

All-Seater Stadiums – or ASSes – will be "safer, more comfortable and more profitable" we are told. However, just because you're seated doesn't mean you're safe: the 300 deaths after a riot in Peru in 1969 and those in the stand at Bradford testify to that.

MYTH

It is a myth that terraces are unsafe. Around 1,175 million people have attended football matches in Britain since the last war. 189 have died.

The tragedies at Hillsborough, Bumden Park in 1946 and Ibrox Park in 1961 and 1971 were all caused by criminal neglect by the police and the clubs.

At Hillsborough the fences at the front were the killers, but the segregation fence erected by the club stopped fans escaping the crush by moving to the side. In the past much larger crowds filled the same terraces, but without the pens and fences there were no problems.

The real reasons for all the fuss about terraces are not – surprise, surprise – about fans' safety at all.

The authorities hate the solidarity (albeit often twisted), the potential violence and, above all, the class hatred that the terraces exhibit and encourage.

They want our game to be like American Football: a game where ordinary working class fans are priced out by having to pay to sit in expensive seats. They want more executive boxes where yuppies can entertain their clients in luxury surroundings while we have to make do with watching the game at home on the box (as long as you can afford satellite TV, of course).

They will be quite happy to see the smaller, less glamourous clubs go broke because they want to destroy football as a working class sport.

The imposition of all-seater stadiums is the beginning of the end of the game as we know and love it, and we will have to FIGHT if we want to keep what WE'VE paid for at the turnstiles for over a century.

GIVE I.D. CARDS

THE BOOT!

*LET'S PLAY SUB-BOOT-EO
WITH THE MINIATURE
FOR SPORT!*

KICK EM
where it hurts

Electric fences, identity cards, alcohol bans. Yeah, football hooliganism hits the headlines again. It's funny how the state and the fucking media sheep who follow them start bleating as soon as their beloved police force face some working class anger, as in the Millwall v. Luton game. Then they bring out their 'war cabinet' and the rest of their loony ideas, but you don't hear a squeak out of them when it's working class people getting razored up or kicked to shit on the terrances.

Which brings me to this point, just what the fuck are we doing? I don't give a fuck about who's the hardest crew, whether it's the Inter-city firm, the Newcastle mainline express, the Leeds service crew, or the Portsmouth 6.57 crew or, on and on and on.

It's a total load of bollocks, all the time we're rucking each other, instead of them, they're laughing at us, because they've got us exactly where they want us, at the bottom of the shit heap. Every time you crack someone who's exactly the same as you, except they support the other team, you might as well be kicking yourself in the head, because you're doing their fucking job for them. The only time the working class has ever achieved anything is when we've stuck together, and taken what we need off the rich scum. There's some brilliant things that happen at football, like rucking the police and looting from shops, but it's time to go a step further, like thieving off the rich instead of each other, hitting the bastards where it really hurts.

Class War
Not Race War

KICK THE RACISTS OUT!

WE HAD A "cracking" time the other Saturday so we thought we'd drop you a line and tell you about it . . .

About 2,000 anti-nazis scared the shit out of the BNP, and the police, on Saturday December 8th. In what was dubbed a "riot" by the Sunday Mail, 28 people were nicked whilst the police tried to protect the Nazis at a pub where they were holding a "rally".

The Battle of Waterloo St resulted in BNP having to be rescued by police vans, who were to take them out of the city centre.

The looks on their faces, especially their so-called "hard men", told us how much they were shitting it, especially when it rained bricks, bottles and banners on their heads!

CRAWLED

Their Fuhrer, John "plummy voice" Tyndall, wasn't able to make it as his train was stopped due to "inclement weather". But we'll tell you what John, try to come to Glasgow again and you'll get your face taken off.

Prat of the year has got to be BNP Glasgow "leader"

Stephen Sinclair who said before the event: "We've deliberately disinformed all those Reds about our rally. Let them try and find us."

Well scum, we felt the wool had really been pulled over our eyes as we aimed our bricks and bottles at your heads as you were crawling our of the pub later on . . . Ha, Ha, Ha.

No Gulf War, No Gang War, No Race War – we want Class War!

Class War "Scheme Team" – Glasgow.

Asian Class War

Asian Class War supporters in Sheffield write . . . Irrespective of which party of the ruling class is in Parliament, racism is increasing and will increase even further. Deportations will increase, racial attacks will increase. This is our reality today and this will be our reality tomorrow, it is not one of our choice, but one which the economic condition of this country forces upon us.

KICK THE Racists Out

get them out of our communities.

self-defence: not a sport, a necessity.

The parasitic layer of black careerists, opportunist coconuts who are institutionalising our struggle, be they in the patronising racist Labour Party – the race advisors, community relations wallahs, multicultural wallahs, rat wallahs – all these sell-outs are making a living on our people's sufferings. In the critical hour they are nowhere to be seen. It's always courageous youths like the Newham 7 and Eustace Pryce who put their personal safety at risk and take up the defence of our communities.

Over the last few years we have bled and fought. As a result we have hardened as a community, we have demonstrated that we recognise the need, and our ability, and our right, to defend ourselves – be it through campaigns against immigration and nationality laws or on the streets against racist police and fascists. The racist state is attempting to buy off and divert our revolutionary struggle. It is tooling up its repressive police force and it is ruthless in its treatment of our people. We must be equally ruthless and determined to defend our brothers and sisters by whatever means necessary!

"If somebody calls me a Paki, I go to them and kick them in the teeth. I don't often get called names, but when I do I get really angry and hit them. There are some English people in our country and we don't go round calling them names."

Ayesha Ahwad, aged 14.

No WAR...

SLAVES

UNLIKE THE *rest of the British Left, who squeal about "British and US imperialism" in the Gulf, and who seem to think that the sun shines out of Saddam Hussein's arse, we make NO distinctions in this war.* This war is just another bosses' war.

On one side is a power-hungry mad despot, with his eyes set on a Arab Empire, and who doesn't think twice about gassing his own people.

PUT THE BOOT IN!

Ranged against him is a rainbow coalition of countries: from the *US*, eager to show the world who is the real boss; *BRITAIN*, a Tory state ridden with the poll tax, and about to sink under the weight of a recession; right through to *SYRIA*, who hate just about everyone else in the coalition, but are keen to put the boot in to their regional rival, Saddam Hussein!

And what is this mighty force defending? *KUWAIT.* A country run like it's some sort of semi-feudal society.

Complete with near-slavery, and only 3%, rich males, able to vote! Some democracy that is!

But don't make the mistake of thinking we are pacifists who believe in standing around with candles, or going on "die-in"'s with a load of liberal vicars and social workers!

Soldiers are trained to kill the enemy. We say turn your guns on the REAL enemy, your officers, bosses and rulers!

We say bring the war home to our streets and communities. Let's fight the real enemy, *the class enemy –* THE WAR TO END ALL WARS, THE WAR TO END ALL CLASSES – CLASS WAR!

But the CLASS WAR

TURN THE GUNS ON THE REAL ENEMY!

STOPPING THE ROT

I F THE HOME Office and press had their way, they'd have us believe that all Arabs and Muslims in this country were Saddam Hussein's "fifth column".

WAR BIGOTS

This state-sponsored WAR BIGOTRY has been not so much out of the interests of "national security" (some detainees have long been opponents of Saddam Hussein), but to portray all Arabs/Muslims (and Asians for that matter) as alien enemies.

This brings fear and isolation in Arab and Asian communities, as well as hostility and fear amongst white/non-Asians of an imagined enemy in all Arabs/Asians.

Ranging from attacks on mosques, deportations and detainments, Arab scaremongering in the press, to Iraqi kids being asked by their teachers in front of their classmates whether they support Hussein!

This is just some of the shit that Arabs have had to put up with in the atmosphere of war bigotry. The scars of this war will probably be long-lasting worldwide.

We've got to get off our arses and help Asians defend their communities against racism; whether it be state racism or organised and unorganised racial attacks – now and beyond our government's war fever.

We need to smash racist beliefs and actions BY ANY MEANS NECESSARY, and promote social solidarity between the different ethnic groups in our class.

STEP UP THE CLASS WAR – BOLLOCKS TO THE RACE WAR.

We Won't Rest Until The Last Benny Hill Has Been STRUNG UP With The Guts Of The Last Bernard Manning

Well over one in three women get raped in Britain. Obviously most people feel absolute disgusted by this, but most of us still believe that rape is an 'isolated act' committed by 'maniacs' and 'loonies' down back alleys. This is the lie regularly told to us by the press and TV. If you believed the papers and TV you'd have the idea that most rapists were nutters who just flipped one day and that they dress up in balaclavas and attack their victims with knives and guns. By doing this the media are trying to convince us that rapists must be 'mad'. This is very far from the truth.

Rape and all violent acts agaisnt women are the NATURAL outcome of a sick, sexist society that sees women as the property of men. The vast majority of rapes are committed by people who the victims know: 'friends', brothers, fathers, husbands, etc. Most rapes do not happen down back alleys or in deserted railway stations but in the rapist's or victim's home. Now these rapists, although scum, are not 'mad', or 'loonies'. They have simply fallen for all the lies spewed on men since we were born. They see themselves as superior and think that every woman is there to be had, to be dominated. In saying this I'm not trying to excuse anybody, all rapists should be murdered without a doubt. But men aren't born rapists; this society deliberately puts the ideas into men's heads that lead to rape.

From 'porno mags' and the adverts on TV, to 'Woman's Own' and Barbara Cartland novels, women are portrayed as dumb, submissive and willing to do anything for men. When kids are young, boys and girls do the same things, play the same games and there's no trouble. It's only as they get older, start copying Mum and Dad and acting out the roles they are told to perform by EVERYTHING they see: books, church, family life, TV, films, advertising etc., that things start to go wrong. Girls think they have to be meek and mild, and look pretty for men to be real women and to be normal. Boys think they have to be tough and hard, and dominate and bully women to be real men and to be normal.

What this vile brainwashing produces is the idea that women enjoy being dominated/assaulted/raped or the attitude of 'what the fuck, she was only a slag anyway'. A good example of the sort of diseased mind this bullshit produces occurred a few years back when a judge said that a woman who'd been brutally raped, was 'asking for it' because she had been hitch-hiking on her own. Another excuse men make is to blame the woman for 'Leading me on', 'laughing at me' or wearing 'revealing clothes'. The times I've heard this shite! If you're so screwed up that you can't control yourself because a woman is wearing a short skirt, that's your problem not hers. Do us all a favour and hang yourself. How would you like it if your wife, girlfriend, sister or mother was raped or assaulted because she was supposedly 'leading him on', 'laughing at him' or whatever the pathetic excuse? Where I work we've got one prick who'll read the papers and say that 'rapists should be hung' and that he 'can't understand them' and then he'll spend the rest of the day reading porno mags, shouting at women from the safety of his van, pinching women's assess etc.

Rape is not an isolated act, it is the last act in a line of insulting behaviour and violence against women: 'wolf whistles', leering, shouting sexist 'jokes', pinching, grabbing, forced kissing, forced touching, assaulting, forced intercourse. Every man is guilty some where along this line, and every woman has suffered somewhere along it also.

The blatant hypocrisy of those who exploit our ignorances and fears of each other (for their own ends) can be found in the pages of such rags as the Sun, where side by side you can have a picture of a model putting on a submissive, dumb pose inviting you to say stuff like 'I wouldn't mind giving her one', side by side to a shock, horror story of a rape. The other despicable trick the press play on us is to describe attacks on women as 'fondlings' 'touching up' and to call rape a 'sexual act'. The journalists who write such things are as guilty of rape as the rapists themselves and they must both be made to suffer the same fate – death.

Rape and assault of women have NOTHING to do with sex. Rape is about DOMINATION. It is about men dominating women. This is why the two most vulnerable sections of the female population, the old and young, are quite often the victims of the rapist. Why else do four month old baby girls and ninety year old pensioners get attacked? Rape is about men who compensate for their own pathetic feelings of inferiority and attack women who they are told by the church, press and TV are inferior to them: wives, girlfriends, sisters or women who can't fight back, young girls and old women. IT HAS NOTHING TO DO WITH SEX!

The press, in its attempt to stay in control, describes anyone who is opposed to seeing women as sex objects for men to own, as 'prudes' and 'anti-sex'. They try to lump us all in with mentally unstable people like Mary Whitehouse and Barbara Cartland. There is nothing wrong with sex; there is nothing wrong with naked bodies; but there IS something wrong with presenting women as brainless pieces of meat for men's use. What upsets people like Whitehouse and Cartland is people having a good fuck, not sexism. In fact arseholes like these encourage sexism with all their puritanical and reactionary 'keep women in the kitchen' garbage.

This leads us to my last point. Contrary to what most middle class feminists think, there can be no great union of 'sisters' between middle class and working class women because, despite all the hassles put upon them by working class men, working class women will, time and time again, stick with their menfolk rather than stomach patronising insults from their so-called middle class 'sisters'. This is because middle class women can NEVER understand what it is to be a working class woman. The answer for working class women combatting sexism and woman-hating lies in organising THEMSELVES with no help from ANY middle class do-gooders. It also requires working class MEN to do something about it: from cutting down the amount of shit they force women to put up with, to physically stopping others who still think it's 'funny' and 'big' to hassle women.

Game For a Laugh

I AM RICH... I MUST SUFFER ONLY IN MY DREAMS

AS FOR THE WORKERS THEY MUST SUFFER ALL THE TIME

In their private lives they flout their public moralising - getting their rocks off by the fantasy of punishment by paying for Sado sex when we should be punishing them in reality on the streets

The state profits in keeping poor people in unhappy situations. This is common knowledge. But in no escape route from poverty is the state more vicious in its punishments, both mental and physical, than with prostitution. The state employs thousands of people, in one form or another, to snoop, arrest and harrass us. While newspapers ensure the rest of the population will despise us. All seeming to join forces to make us crack.

Although prostitution is not illegal in itself, soliciting and advertising are. Which makes it a bit fucking awkward without telepathy. But if prostitutes were illegal it would mean the punters would get done too for participating in a crime. And that means pigs and judges and peers of the realm. The same men who make the laws which they say are to protect us from pimps and unscrupulous criminals, when usually the only men to get money out of us is this selfsame bunch of lawmaking creeps.

To dwell on pimps and ponces is exactly what the state wants, and that is to reaffirm that no "decent" man would go out with a whore. And if he does he can get locked up for it. Yet another law to keep us alone and vulnerable.

CASH FOR A CHANGE

We appreciate working as necessary for survival, but as anarchists appreciate all work as prostitution. If we are going to be subjected to "work" we must earn the most amount possible for the least amount of work. Which for most women means prostitution.

SIMPLE MINDS

There is though within the women's movement open hostility to prostitutes which prevents any open discussion. Those of us who have gone through the women's movement to fight back against our circumstances have often felt despair at coming up against a brick wall of criticism and prejudice, especially galling when it comes from women we had thought were educated and thinking enough to see through the propaganda.

But they reckon without our strength. We are a section of the class who are not allowing circumstances to wash over us. We have tasted poverty, now we take responsibility for our lives.

Which also means we will not let the little Hitlers of the womens movement walk over us. They are used to working class women being in awe of them. But we know what middle class authority is built on from our punters – FUCK ALL.

The reasons given against the profession though are of course ideological. But when this criticism comes from some cow doing a sociology degree, we know who's got the moral job. 'Cos in a few years time she'll have clients too. It's just all hers will be under age and have no choice about seeing her.

Recently our left wing sisters on Camden council have set up a centre to rehabilitate us. Now it is no fun working on the street but if you are working class as well it is virtually impossible to get off, even with money. Landlords and agents are instantly suspicious of a single working class girl with money, and suss on to what you are up to. So are you gonna rehabilitate me in a flat? So you have set up a centre to rehabilitate me. At what?! Like, how about some of that money you get for telling me what to do, scum. Sitting there suggesting I try a little light factory work.

Huh, you sitting there wearing a "woman's right to choose" badge:

I don't choose oppression, sister.

I don't choose to send people to factories for a ton a week.

I don't choose for one of your sister social workers to take my kids.

But I may choose to meet you after work one night.

So quit the do-gooding, sisters. We've been on the streets a long time. WE KNOW the impossibility of working in any movement controlled by the middle class. They willl stop at nothing to cling onto their power, even at the expense of their original aims and ideals. We know there is no recession. We see the money. These rich bastards spend more on a quick wank than they see fit to award us per week on the dole.

THE ONLY WAY TO CHANGE THE ORDER OF THINGS IS WITH CLASS WAR, LED BY THE CLASS.

Using Sisterhood Like The Masons Use Brotherhood

The wimmins liberation movement is riddled with the bourgeoisie. These middle class trendies are dominating every wimmins group and organisation. Are we really expected to tolerate these reformist turds? Why should we put up with "well off" scum making a living off the backs of working class wimmin? Stuff their mysticism – we as anarchists have not the time nor patience to tolerate this rubbish. How many of us can afford to spend hours in self-indulging bullshit about our relationship to the moon and the glories of childbirth? When I have a period it fucking hurts and I don't give a shit about my relationship to the moon. And tell a working class woman, struggling to bring up kids, about the glories of childbirth and she will probably tell you to "PISS OFF", and why shouldn't she? It might not be that she doesn't want to know about wimmins liberation but who wants to know in those unrealistic terms?

Are we really supposed to be able to afford these glossy wimmins press and virago classics? Well I can't fucking afford £5 for a book. Rip them off and take the money back off the bourgeois feminists. Let's have some class consciousness in our movement. Smash the hierarchies the middle class feminists are building.

Not long ago I tried to get involved in a group of wimmin who supposedly "help" the working class wimmin; or do they help themselves? I found they were all "doing quite nicely thank you very much". And easing their social consciences at the same time. This is nothing unusual!

We as anarchist wimmin should either let them rot together or do it all ourselves, but we will not be "led" (sic) or be expected to tolerate these bastards.

I don't feel affiliated to these wimmin, in fact I feel embarrassed by them. As an anarchist when you walk into a circle of wimmin wearing trendy cashmere jumpers and chic "feminist" boots all relating to each other maaan. And when the leader (sic) of the meeting suggests that we all get to know each other by going round in a circle and saying a bit about ourselves and our names, doesn't it make you want to stand up and vomit all over their jumpers?

These wimmin use sisterhood like the masons use brotherhood – for self-interest, money and power.

Fuck SPUC

As the climate of the "new morality" hots up, it is obvious that working class women and teenage girls are going to get most fucked over by it.

Abortion is a difficult and traumatic experience at the best of times without these middle class do-gooders trying to interfere. They tell you that abortion is murder even when the fertilised egg is little bigger than a pea. Every month our bodies get rid of thousands of eggs – what is that? Mass murder? No, it's a period and before you know it they'll be trying to ban our periods! As women we must be able to make our own decisions about our own bodies and cannot allow these decisions to be taken away from us.

In many ways abortion is a class issue. We are the women who can't afford to have one kid after another, even if we wanted. Then the harder it is for women to get abortion, the more working class women suffer. Rich women have always been able to get safe abortions; we cannot afford to pay for abortions at private clinics. Although we can get abortions on the NHS, we are often treated like shit. We are patronized and called "silly girls" for not being more responsible about contraception; they seem to forget that there is no completely safe and effective method of contraception.

Look at these self-appointed guardians of the nation's morality – are any of them working class? And certainly none of them are teenagers. No, these middle class scum live in nice warm houses with nice big gardens for the children to play in. They have the soup kitchen mentality, pat us on the head from time to time and keep an eye on our very dubious morality. They want to keep us on the straight and narrow. Why? Because it's just another way of controlling us and patronizing us, and there's nothing they enjoy more than preaching at us from their nice homes in the countryside, while we sit and have yet another decision taken away from our hands.

They know what's best for us after all. The hypocritical morality of such organisations as SPUC, LIFE, the churches, etc. takes on outstanding proportions. While condemning women who seek abortions, they are invariably the same people who at the same time condemn single parents.

BEHOLD Your Future Executioners

A woman and child freeze to death in a south London council flat; on the south coast when a disabled woman freezes to death in temporary homeless family accommodation her six year old child puts his own clothes on his mother's dead body to keep her warm and lives off stale christmas cake for two days. How much more of this fuckin horrible shit society are we going to take?

Old people lie in bed all day – it's the only way to keep warm – they can't even afford to put the one bar electric fire on and many freeze to death; kidney patients die because there aren't enough dialysis machines – doctors are told to decide who should get treatment on grounds of social standing, job, wealth, etc. – the poor die, the rich get treated; children are burnt to death in the upstairs bedrooms of council homes – the firemen discover that the only lighting in the house was candles because the electricity had been cut off; striking miners die under roof cave-ins as they scrabble for lumps of coal on slag heaps.

Meanwhile in the very same towns that these events take place in almost daily the rich flaunt their lives of luxury in our faces. Their huge swanky mansions, their flash Rolls Royces, their posh dinner parties – they spend more on one piece of jewellery or fur coat than whole families have to struggle to survive on for years. Well now is the time to bring some reality into their complacent lives – we aim to bring the class war home to these bloated rich bastards.

Every town in Britain has its rich and poor areas and we aren't going to keep out of sight and mind in our shitty council estates any longer. We're going to march into the rich areas and put the shits up these scumbags... there's going to be a whole lot of BASH THE RICH marches all over the country.

The idea of bash the rich marches is nothing new. Exactly 100 years ago on April 28 1885 they were doing exactly the same thing in Chicago. The conditions under which the working class lived there were appalling – here's a contemporary account: "There were rooms lighted only by the cracks in the wall, water closets full of excrement, entire families sick, children slowly starving to death, ice cold rooms with no fire in the stove. The winter was one of the coldest, most bitter in Chicago's history.

Families built fires in empty lots at night, trying to keep warm in their thin and torn jackets. Thousands died of hunger or froze to death. Many bodies had been found floating in Lake Michigan the previous winter – the last remains of people who decided it was better to die quickly rather than slowly by starvation."

At the same time huge fortunes were beng made by factory owners paying slave labour wages and dining sumptously in restaurants in the rich parts of the city. The anarchist Lucy Parsons told people who were on the verge of killing themselves to "take a few rich people with you", let their eyes be opened to see what was going on "by the red glare of destruction." Anarchists would hold huge meetings attended by up to 20,000 people. At one Lucy Parsons said "let every dirty, lousy tramp arm himself with a revolver or knife and lay in wait on the steps of the palaces of the rich and stab or shoot their owners as they come out. Let us devastate the avenues where the wealthy live."

The anarchists led huge marches from the working class ghettos in to the rich neighbourhoods. They would gather in thousands outside restaurants or the homes of the wealthy displaying a huge banner on which was written "BEHOLD YOUR FUTURE EXECUTIONERS", the terrified rich would summon the police and huge riots would take place. The working class of Chicago were determined to take their struggle into the heart of the enemies' territory – so are we, a hundred years later.

CLASS WAR Now

hen *Class War* started back in the early 80's no one could have foreseen what it would grow into. Originally the paper was a hard attack on the 60's and 70's forms of rebellion – fuck love and peace, get out on the streets and fight back! The paper unashamedly poured out it's hatred for the rich scum that controlled our lives, and those that protected them. It came right out and said things that others wouldn't even dream of.

The paper seized upon something that the Left had failed to understand – class hatred. People who read *Class War* found it uniquely refreshing after the staid politics of the boring, "established", middle class, trendy Left.

The articles in *Class War* slagged off pacifism and the Peace movement and encouraged the idea that violence is necessary. They put forward a straightforward analysis, identifying the enemy not only as "the system" or "the State", but as the ruling class (not only as a class, but also as individuals).

When the Miner's strike started in 1984, the paper and its followers reacted swiftly. The writers of earlier issues of *Class War* had wanted to see the Anarchist/punk ghetto take up the rebellion unleashed by the inner-city riots of 1981. Now that anger was taken up by thousands of miners throughout the country. To a large extent the paper dropped its discussion of the inadequacies of the CND and called for direct physical support for the miners. *Class War* alone supported the direct action of the strikers. Readership soared, not least in mining areas . . . miners queued 20 or more for the paper at the big Mansfield demonstration in 1984. *Class War* was now a paper with readers and supporters well beyond the wildest expectations of its founders.

Soon *Class War* became more than a paper. People around the country wanted to be part of this new and honest political movement. In the early days Class War consisted of only 50 or so people but its impact was magnified a hundred fold.

Class War had an effect on the political and cultural climate in the late 80's. We predicted that the 'old' traditional ways of class struggle were on the way out, if not already dead. The government had beaten the unions and they were ready to take us on in our own com-

munities. Our straightforward no-nonsense class politics stirred up already existing hatred in the hearts of working class people. Instead of the Yuppie being the envy of the working class, *Class War* targeted these parasites and made "Yuppie" a dirty word.

At this time *Class War* was no more than a paper, with a loose collective of people behind it. But those who eagerly read *Class War* wanted more than just a paper, they wanted a new political movement that would reflect the politics of working class revolution and self-management. This pressure built up until finally the Class War Federation was born.

Since then the Federation has evolved until the point where we are now a membership organisation, with a constitution and real democracy, where all members have an equal vote. There are no "leaders" and all delegates are instantly recallable. This is in stark contrast to what usually happens when a tiny group of people get together and launch a political party, present a platform of ideas to people and tell them to like it or lump it! "Kick out the Tories" they say, "so we can take their place" – Bollocks. We aren't interested in getting rid of one set of bosses only to replace them with another.

The destruction of the state socialist countries in the late 80's, and early 90's focussed people's attention upon methods of political organisation like never before. They started to see state socialism for what it was, dictatorship by another name. Meanwhile the capitalist countries were nosediving into yet another round of war, recession and unemployment. Interest in our politics grew rapidly until we reached a point where, on the Poll Tax "victory" demo in March 1991, thousands of people marched with us. Sales of our propaganda sky-rocketed – in one month alone we flogged over 250,000 stickers!

One thing is certain: Our rulers will not give up their power without a bloody fight, we must take on capitalism and the state if we are to realise our ambitions of a better world. To do this we must come together to form organisations that are capable of changing the whole system.

The Class War Federation is the most dynamic, ambitious and popular of these organisations. As the class war hots up nationally and internationally we ask you to join the resistance. Don't sit on the sidelines – join the winning side!

CLASS WAR on

the streets of LONDON

membership form

I'm already a supporter...and quite honestly CLASS WAR could do with me as a member!

NAME ....

ADDRESS ....
....

FILL OUT AND RETURN THIS FORM AND YOUR LOCAL ORGANISER WILL CONTACT YOU ABOUT BECOMING A MEMBER.
SEND TO: The National Secretaries, PO BOX 39, Manchester M15 5HN.

paper subscription

PLEASE SEND ME THE NEXT:
❑ TURBO SUB (COST £10.00)
❑ 12 ISSUES (COST £5.00)
❑ 6 ISSUES (COST £2.50) *OF CLASS WAR*

TURBO SUB IS A SUPPORTERS SUB : YOU GET 6 ISSUES, A COPY OF THE HEAVY STUFF, A COPY OF THIS IS CLASS WAR, 3 BACK ISSUES, STICKERS AND A BADGE !

Cheques etc. payable to CLASS WAR.
Send to: CW, PO bOX 772, Bristol BS99 1EG.

TO: NAME...
ADDRESS...
....

FREE BADGE AND BACK ISSUE WITH EVERY NEW SUB !

from issue No. ☐ With my first issue please send me 1 back issue, number: ☐ (issues 26-48 only) Turbo Sub choose 3

Heavy Stuff subscription

DO THE RIGHT THING! SUBSCRIBE TO THE HEAVY STUFF CLASS WAR'S THEORETICAL/DISCUSSION MAGAZINE.

❑ £6.00 FOR 4 ISSUES
❑ HERE'S £10 - KEEP THE CHANGE AND BUY A DICTIONARY!

Please send to: **NAME** ....
ADDRESS...

SEND TO: PO BOX 1QF, NEWCASTLE-U-TYNE, NE 99 1QF.
CHEQUES PAYABLE TO HEAVY STUFF

Printed in the United States
by Baker & Taylor Publisher Services